Dedicated to

the memory of Margaret LaHaye,
Bible student, soulwinner,
Child Evangelism director in
Lansing, Michigan, for 23 years,
and my mother.

Her love for Bible prophecy
sparked my own. She went
to be with her Lord last year—
and now all her questions
are answered, for she "knows
even as she is known."

CONTENTS

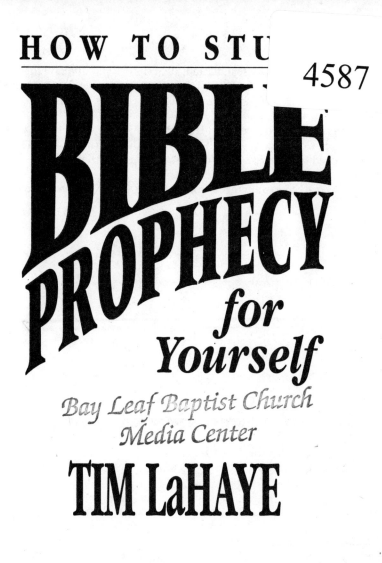

HOW TO STUDY

BIBLE PROPHECY

for Yourself

*Bay Leaf Baptist Church
Media Center*

TIM LaHAYE

HARVEST HOUSE PUBLISHERS
Eugene, Oregon 97402

HOW TO STUDY BIBLE PROPHECY FOR YOURSELF

Copyright © 1990 by Tim LaHaye
Published by Harvest House Publishers
Eugene, Oregon 97402

Library of Congress Cataloging-in-Publication Data

LaHaye, Tim F.
    How to study Bible prophecy for yourself / Tim LaHaye.
    ISBN 0-89081-817-7
    1. Bible—Prophecies.   2. Bible—Study.   I. Title.
  BS647.2.L34   1990   90-36388
  225.1'5—dc20   CIP

Printed in the United States of America.

THE URGENCY

After a decade of disinterest in Bible prophecy, mankind's fascination with the future has begun exploding, until prophecy has now become a necessity in the life of every believer. "The signs of the times" are everywhere! Satanism is on the rise, even invading some of our public schools, where the Bible has been expelled. Consequently, vulnerable children and youth do not have access to the one Book that warns them of Satanism's dangers and gives them competent guidance on how to avoid its harmful influence.

Earthquakes, another "sign of the end of the age," have reached unprecedented proportions. More deaths and devastation by earthquakes were recorded during the past decade than at any time in the history of man. Remember the quakes in Mexico, Albania, China, and San Francisco? Seismologists (scientists who study earthquakes) suspect that our earth is twisting and gyrating at its core in anticipation of the greatest earthquake in world history, which is why millions who live near the San Andreas fault, which runs almost the length of California, worry that it could strike any day. The California State Legislature is so concerned that it will come soon that they are contemplating requiring home-owners to carry special earthquake insurance. Bible prophecy predicts that just such a cataclysmic earthquake is yet to come (see Revelation chapter 6).

What about famines in Egypt, Africa, China, and various Third World countries? These too were prophesied in the Bible as signs of the end.

And, in spite of the incredible advances in modern medicine, we have the devastating plagues of sexually transmitted diseases, cancer, and the 100 percent fatal virus of AIDS, not to mention the new and stronger strains of gonorrhea that do not respond to wonder drugs. Plagues too are a sign of the end, as are drugs, murder, rebellion of children against parents—and the list goes on.

And now we have the geopolitical phenomenon that no one expected: the rupture of Communism and the amazing worldwide spread of the quest for democracy. This is creating an ideal climate for the fulfillment of the century-old dream of the intellectually elite who reject God: A ONE-WORLD GOVERNMENT. Who can deny its potential in view of the globalism and New Age philosophy of public school textbooks, not only in this country but in many countries on both sides of the torn Communist curtain? But that should not surprise the knowledgeable student of prophecy. The Bible tells us that a one-world dictator called "Antichrist" is going to arise who will rule the world in the last days.

On top of all this, the odometer on the world's calendar will soon roll over to the year 2000 A.D. and we will be plunged into a whole new millennium. Without question "millennial fever" will sweep the world, and false messiahs and false prophets will arise "deceiving even the very elect" if Christians are not careful.

Our Lord said, "Let no man deceive you" when these things come. The only way to avoid being deceived is to know your Bible, particularly Bible prophecy.

Jesus Christ is coming again! Even many people who are not Christians believe that fact, according to a recent Gallup poll on religion. We can't know "the day or the hour" but we can know "the season" or general period of time. And we should all be prepared for Christ when He comes.

That's what this book is all about—to acquaint you with God's wonderful plan for the future so you won't be deceived by false teachers and charlatans who come in sheep's clothing but who lead many Christians astray. You will see that the best days for mankind are yet ahead.

Prophecy is not so difficult that we can't understand it, or else God would not have put it into Scripture. This book is written to help you find out for yourself what God has in store for you in both your earthly and your eternal future.

You will find it both exciting and inspiring, and I pray that it will motivate you to live every day as if your Lord could return to this earth momentarily as He promised and take you to be with Him, permitting you to become an eyewitness and participant in His exciting plan for the future of mankind.

This is not an ordinary book. You don't just read it, but you also *study* it. It can help you find out for yourself what you believe prophecy teaches. It is a companion to my other study book by Harvest House Publishers, *How to Study the Bible for Yourself.*

The book you are now reading will give you a working knowledge of the basics in Bible prophecy and the study of future things. It will equip you to answer the false teachers that are popping up everywhere. Even more important, it will help you straighten out the thinking of the many people you meet who are being deceived by them.

The Bible challenges us to "rightly divide the Word of Truth." This book will help you rightly divide the truths of prophecy!

CHAPTER 1

A New Way to Study Prophecy

✦

You are about to embark on an exciting but sometimes controversial Bible study—one that could change your life. Actually, prophecy sometimes becomes controversial because there are so many different opinions about it. Most of the controversy is over such things as the timing of the Lord's return or the interpretation of signs related to it. Rather than be labeled "controversial," some Bible teachers rarely or never teach prophecy, even though it occupies one-third of all Scripture.

A popular Bible teacher taught his congregation the entire New Testament book by book, from Matthew to Jude. The next week he started in again at the book of Matthew. One of his students interrupted him and said, "You have forgotten the book of Revelation" (an entire book of prophecy). The teacher responded, "Oh, it's too controversial and too difficult to understand."

This is no time in history to avoid "the study of future things," which is what prophecy is. If we avoid teaching Christians the basics about prophecy, they will be "tossed to and fro" by false teachers who come to them with cunningly devised fables and interpretations that will deceive them. And if our expectations are correct, that increase of false teachers has already come on the scene and will increase between now and the next century. Christians need to know *more* about prophecy, not less, for that is the only way for them to be armed with the truth.

It is this author's conviction, after studying prophecy for many years, and after writing four books on the subject (including a commentary on the book of Revelation), that prophecy is not so difficult to understand that it should be avoided. Instead, it could be dangerous to the spiritual health of Christians to avoid it. The apostle Paul obviously thought prophecy was important for young Christians to study, for he addressed it in every chapter in the little book of 1 Thessalonians. (Bible scholars tell us that this five-chapter book was probably the very first of his 13 epistles to be written, and that Paul had ministered in Thessalonica for only three weeks, yet obviously had taught many prophetic things during that short time.) In 1 Thessalonians 5:1-5 we read:

> Now, brothers, about times and dates we do not need to write to you, for you know very well that the day of the Lord will come like a thief in the night. While people are saying "Peace and safety," destruction will come on them suddenly, as labor pains on a pregnant woman, and they will not escape.
>
> But you, brothers, are not in darkness so that this day should surprise you like a thief. You are all sons of the light and sons of the day. We do not belong to the night or to the darkness (NIV).

Obviously Paul did not think that such a subject as "the day of the Lord" (another reference to the second coming of Christ) was too complex for these baby Christians. The fourth chapter of 1 Thessalonians, which we will study later, contains the most detailed description of the coming of Christ for His church to be found in the whole Bible. Then in 2 Thessalonians, which was written just a short time later, Paul taught about the coming of the Antichrist and other future events. Paul obviously did not think that future subjects were too controversial or so hard to understand that they should be ignored. Instead, he considered them important for young believers, and especially essential to challenge Christians to live holy lives in an unholy age.

Some details of prophecy are admittedly difficult to understand, but the essentials are not. And that is why this book is written—to help you see by your own study that such subjects as the return of our Lord, the resurrection of the dead, the future activities of the dead (including the judgment seat of Christ for Christians only and the white throne judgment for sinners only), the millennial kingdom, heaven, and the glorious appearing of Christ to rule and reign over this earth (as well as other related subjects) are just not that hard to understand.

I am convinced that even if some minor misunderstanding results from the pursuit of prophetic studies, this is still far better than ignoring the whole subject. Ignorance has never been a virtue! As the apostle Paul said, "I would not have you ignorant, brethren." I share that concern. I would not have you ignorant about the most important events that God has planned for your future. For if you understand His plan, it will motivate you to live the kind of life that will cause Him to say to you on judgment day, "Well done, good and faithful servant; enter into the joy of your Lord."

THE UNIQUENESS OF THIS STUDY

Most books on prophecy, including my others, are written by one or more authors for the purpose of persuading you of their own interpretation of the prophetic Scriptures. However, the purpose of this book is to help you analyze the prophetic passages of the New Testament (and those from the Old Testament that have a bearing on them) in such a way that you can come to your own conclusions. Scripture texts will be given with space available for you to write your own understanding from the passage. Questions will be asked to help you reach your own conclusions. This way God can speak to you directly on the subject. Then *after* you have reached your own conclusion on what you believe the text teaches, I will provide my understanding of it for comparison. In some cases I will also give other interpretations by Bible-believing Christians for you to consider.

Keep in mind that the Bible was not written to divide Christians, even though it has sometimes been used that way. (In some instances, whole denominations were started over prophetic differences.) The Bible was written to ordinary people like you and me. Most passages are easy to understand and believe if we apply the "golden rule of interpretation" to the passage: *"When the plain sense of Scripture makes common sense, seek no other sense, but take every word at its primary, literal meaning, unless the facts of the immediate context clearly indicate otherwise."* As the apostle John said in Scripture about Christians understanding God's Word for themselves:

> These things I have written to you concerning those who try to deceive you. But the anointing which you have received from Him abides in you, and you do not need that anyone teach you; but as the same anointing teaches you concerning all things, and this is true, and is not a lie, and just as it has taught you, you will abide in Him (1 John 2:26,27).

If you are a Christian you can understand the Bible, including the prophecy passages, and especially those verses that God designed to motivate His children to live holy lifestyles. Our Lord promised, "When the Spirit of truth is come, He will guide you into all truth...and He will tell you what is to come."

But first, let's examine *why Christians should study prophecy.*

CHAPTER 2

Why Christians Should Study Prophecy

◆

God has given us three important signs that He is a supernatural God. The first is creation, the second is Jesus Christ, His Son, and the third is His written revelation of Himself that we call the Bible.

Creation provides ample evidence that He exists (Romans 1:19,20). Because it is totally impossible to get order out of disorder, only a blatant skeptic would deny that the magnificent order in this well-designed universe demands some Superdesigner. All creation testifies that there was a God of creative design behind this universe and this earth, including mankind.

Jesus Christ, the most famous and influential man who ever lived, is the evidence of both God's existence and His incredible love for mankind. For He not only sent His Son into this world to identify with mankind, but to *die* for mankind, so that men and women could have their sins forgiven and then enjoy God forever.

But the very best revelation we have is the Bible. Creation is limited in what it can tell us about God; it does not reveal His love or His forgiveness—only His almighty power. Jesus the Son is the complete revelation of God for His words and actions, and His teachings were the exact expression of God. Yet they were dependent on the written Word of God for preservation and present-day discussion. We would know very little about Christ if it were not for the Bible.

Within the Bible we have a whole body of truth that testifies to the divine authorship of Scripture, and that body of truth is *fulfilled prophecy*. Only God can foretell the future. Man tries, but in time he is shown to be a fraud. D. James Kennedy, in one of his messages, tells of reading 50 prophecies in *Enquirer* magazine that were to happen in the 1970's. By the time the 1980's came to pass, not one of them had been fulfilled!

The Bible, however, is filled with prophecies that have come to pass—prophecies about Israel, about the Gentile nations, and most important of all, about the Messiah. The fact of fulfilled prophecy is how we can know without a doubt that Jesus Christ is the Messiah of God: Over 100 prophecies of His first coming were fulfilled in His birth, life, and death!

And that is why we can be so confident that He is coming again. In fact, someone has counted eight times as many prophecies regarding Christ's *second* coming as for His *first* coming! But as comforting and exciting as that certainty is, it will be of no help to the Christian unless he studies it for himself, or it is taught to him by someone else. There are, of course, other reasons as well for studying this very impor tant subject. Consider the following.

1. *God must consider prophecy important, for He has put so much of it in the Bible.*

The Bible is not a single book but is actually a library of books which contain almost one-third prophetic writings. Of God's 66 volumes to mankind, you will find that most of the books were written by prophets. Even Moses, the lawgiver and author of the first five books of the Old Testament, was a prophet. Samuel, Elijah, Daniel, John the Baptist—in fact, most of God's messengers to man to reveal

His plan—were prophets. In the New Testament, there was a special first-century gift known as the "gift of prophecy." Peter, Paul, James, Jude, and others had that gift. Our Lord, of course, knew all things, and He gave the most definitive prophecy of things still to come in His Olivet Discourse. There are 16 books on prophecy in the Old Testament, including the Minor and the Major Prophets. In the New Testament, God used four books to cover the subject— Revelation, 1 and 2 Thessalonians, and Jude. In addition, many of the other books include long prophetic passages or subjects, such as our Lord's Olivet Discourse in Matthew 24 and 25. Just from the amount of material covered in Scripture called prophecy, it is clear that God intended for His children to study it. If we omit the study of prophecy as too controversial, too difficult, or complex, we will omit almost one-third of the entire Bible!

2. *Prophecy reveals our Lord as He really is.*

One of the reasons I have always loved prophecy is because of the exalted view it gives of our Lord. The prophetic portrayal of Christ is different than that of the Gospels, which tell the wonderful story of His humiliation, including His birth, suffering, and death. In order to "taste death for every man," Christ had to humble Himself and make Himself "lower than the angels"; consequently, He was abused by mankind. It was not a pretty sight to see our Lord abused, rejected, and crucified by His creation.

But the second coming is a different matter! Never again will Jesus Christ come into this world to suffer or be subject to the whims of man. The next time He comes it will be "in power and great glory" as "King of Kings and Lord of Lords." At that coming the Bible says that "every eye shall see Him" (Revelation 1:7 KJV) and that "every knee [shall] bow, of those in heaven, and of those on earth, and of those under the earth, and that every tongue [shall] confess that Jesus Christ is Lord, to the glory of God the Father" (Philippians 2:10,11).

3. *A proper understanding of prophecy arms the believer against cults and false prophets.*

Scripture teaches that false Christs and false teachers will arise in the last days. While there have always been false teachers who have led millions of people astray, as we approach the end times there will be an increase of these devilish attacks on the minds and morals of God's people. The best defense is to "put on the full armor of God so that you can take your stand against the devil's schemes" (Ephesians 6:11 NIV). Our Lord predicted that the false Christs and false prophets that will appear in the end times, some of whom will be able to perform great signs and miracles, will deceive even the elect—that is, believers who do not know the Scriptures, particularly those Scriptures that relate to future things.

A good illustration of this principle in action is the Jehovah's Witnesses, who came on the religious scene at about the turn of the twentieth century. They predicted that a special group of 144,000 witnesses of Jehovah would arise just before the coming of Christ, and they were commissioned to recruit them. Those Christians who understood Revelation 7:5-8 (from which Jehovah's Witnesses claim to get this teaching) were not deceived, for they knew that those 144,000 witnesses would arise during the coming tribulation period, and that all of the witnesses would be Jews. (The Jehovah's Witnesses are primarily Gentiles.) In 1960 the Witnesses realized that they had recruited more people into their membership than 144,000, so they changed their interpretation of prophecy to fit their growth. From then on, they began teaching that only special members who did a lot of witnessing got into the 144,000 that would go to heaven. The rest were promised that they would "inherit the earth."

A more recent illustration is the man who sold 300,000 books explaining his claim that Christ was coming in September of 1988. The date came and went, and he realized he was wrong. So he refigured his teaching and decided he had missed the date by exactly one year—so he put out another book. This one only sold 30,000 copies! Many individuals, on the basis of this false teaching, are said to have sold their homes, quit their jobs, and begun "awaiting the Lord's return." Such Christians would have known better if they had been taught the simple fact in our Lord's prophetic discourse regarding the time of His coming: "Of that day and hour no one knows, no, not even the angels of heaven, but My Father only" (Matthew 24:36).

A good rule to follow about any teacher of prophecy who sets a day or hour for the coming of Christ is: *Don't believe him!* As our Lord said, "Many will come in my name, saying 'I am the Christ,' and will deceive many" (Matthew 24:5). The best way to avoid being deceived by the false teachers that are coming is to know the prophetic teachings of the Word of God.

4. *The study of prophecy promotes an evangelistic church.*

The most evangelistic periods of church history have been times when the church studied prophecy. The church of Thessalonica, which was an infant church that Paul taught the truths of prophecy, was also an evangelistic church. So also was the early church as a whole. From the time that our Lord said, "I will come again and receive you unto myself," the early church had an evangelistic fire that lasted almost three centuries. True, it was a persecuted church, but part of the reason it was persecuted was because of its evangelistic fire that was due in part to the prominent teaching of our Lord's soon return.

Later, when paganism was brought into the church in about the fourth century, the Bible was no longer taught widely. It began to become an object of worship, and that produced the Dark Ages—dark toward the truths of the Word of God, for the Bible was put into museums but not read. That is why John Wycliffe (1330–1384) is considered one of the greatest Christian leaders of all time. In the fourteenth century he determined to translate the Word of God into the common language so that everyone could read it for himself. He was called "the morning star of the Reformation," and the Bible began to be studied again. In the nineteenth century came the rediscovery of the study of prophecy, or the study of last things. It was during this period that the greatest missionary and evangelistic emphasis of the modern church era was born. Throughout the past century some of the most evangelistic and missionary-minded churches were those that taught prophecy, especially the prophecies of our Lord's soon return.

One practical area where this is helpful is in counteracting the materialism of this present age. I need not convince the reader of this book that we live in a materialistic age that is not conducive to sacrifice or spiritual dedication. But the reality which the person who studies Bible prophecy receives is that this world is very temporary. One day "all these things will be burned up," and, as the Scripture asks, "Then whose shall these things be?" The Christian untaught in prophetic truth is prone to get the idea that "all things continue as they were . . . where is the promise of His coming?" But the promise is there; it just needs to be found in the study of prophecy.

5. *The study of prophecy tends to purify the believer.*

It is no secret that we live in an unholy age. Unfortunately, too much of that unholiness is found even in the church. One tool which the Holy Spirit uses to help believers live holy lives is the study of prophecy, particularly those passages that relate to our Lord's soon return. As the apostle John said of those who had the promise of the Lord's second coming in their hearts: "Everyone who has this hope in Him purifies himself, just as He is pure" (1 John 3:3).

Many a believer, including this writer, has in a moment of temptation thought, "Do I want to be doing this when

Christ returns?" When the answer is a resounding "NO!" it is easier to reject the temptation. Instead, we are challenged to so live that when He comes we will be found doing those things that will earn His praise, "Well done, good and faithful servant," rather than the rebuke that will be extended to those who are "ashamed before Him at His coming." It is my prayer that the study of the exciting prophecies we shall examine in this book will produce a heightened degree of holiness in your life so that you will be ready when He comes.

6. *Prophecy offers confident hope in a hopeless age.*

Human beings can absorb many pressures in life, but lack of hope is not one of them. The world in which we live has no hope. Looking back, we see an unending history of war, war, war, all of which reveals the inhuman traits of mankind. The very study of history is a study of war and man's inhumanity to his fellowman. Yet the whole world yearns for peace, but knows no peace. Even the world's greatest thinkers have no workable solutions to the myriad problems facing humankind. Prophecy students, however, not only know what our loving God has planned for the future of this planet and the billions who live on it, but they have a firm confidence (that is the biblical definition of "hope") toward the future and are not afraid. We can say, "If we live, praise the Lord. If we die, praise the Lord!" Or we can say with the early Christians, "Even so, come, Lord Jesus." They had a greeting that needs to be rekindled in the church today: "Maranatha" (1 Corinthians 16:22), meaning "The Lord is coming." The student of prophecy will not dread the uncertain future, for he not only knows some of the things that "must come to pass" but he also knows the One who holds the future.

The sad part is that the worst days in world history are not behind us but are still ahead. Our Lord Himself warned that toward the end of human history as we have known it there would be a time of "great tribulation, such as has not been since the beginning of the world until this time, no, nor ever shall be" (Matthew 24:21). When we study that passage in detail, we see that this terrifying future will be unparalleled in human history. Yet it should offer no great personal concern for the Christian who rightly understands God's prophetic plan as it is outlined in the Scriptures, for he is confident of his place in God's plan. Unfortunately, many Christians unnecessarily experience the same distress and insecurity that shall come upon the rest of mankind when they go through the things destined to come upon the earth.

This confidence (or "hope," as it is called in Scripture) is not automatic; it comes in response to the study not just of the Word of God in general but of those passages that pertain to prophecy. You may wonder why I keep calling "hope" as it appears in Scripture "confidence." But that is what the biblical word "hope" literally means. Because of our faith in the Lord of the future, which is strengthened by our study of the Word of God, we do not look to the future with a casual meaning for hope: "We hope things will turn out all right." No, we are *confident* that the future will happen exactly as Christ predicted. We do not merely wish that Jesus will come again; we are *confident* that He *will* come again, because He promised He would. The more we know about God's prophetic promises, the more convinced we will become of their future reality.

If, as many prophecy scholars believe, we begin to see world governments begin to merge into one federated government over which one key leader will rule, Christians need not become unduly worried, for that would be just one more sign that the coming of the Lord is near. The same is true in regard to the other signs predicted for the end of the age, such as earthquakes, famines, pestilences, a spirit of lawlessness, and the disintegration of the family. Informed Christians will enjoy a "peace that passes all understanding" as a result of knowing the prophetic word.

Bible prophecy predicts the ultimate destruction of Satan by the Lord Jesus Christ. Currently Satan "is the god of this age" (2 Corinthians 4:4), and that is why it seems that evil continually overcomes good. But prophecy tells us that on the day when Our Lord comes He will chain Satan in the bottomless pit, where he "will tempt the nations no more." And ultimately He will triumph over Satan forever. Christians who know nothing about these future events will have little confidence or hope as they face the future. Those familiar with prophecy are the only ones who can face what seems to be an uncertain future with peaceful confidence.

CHAPTER 3

The Certainty of Christ's Second Coming

✦

One of the most incredible discoveries of George Gallup's surveys of religion was that more than 62 percent of the American people believe that Jesus Christ will return literally to this earth. (The same percentage believe in the unique deity of Christ.) What makes this statistic so amazing is that the same survey indicated that 40 percent of the American people profess a born-again experience with Jesus Christ. In other words, 22 percent more Americans believe in our Lord's second coming than are ready to meet Him when He does come! That in itself should be a tremendous motivation for us to share our faith so that those 22 percent can receive Him. Taken another way, more than two out of every ten people already believe enough about Christ to receive Him personally.

The second coming of Christ, as we have already seen, is mentioned eight times more frequently in the Old and the New Testaments than His first coming. In fact, His second coming is evidently the second-most-important doctrine in the entire New Testament, for the only teaching mentioned more frequently is the subject of salvation!

Second coming teachings are so tied in with almost every other biblical doctrine that Christianity would be destroyed if Christ were never to come back for His church as He promised. His coming is mentioned 318 times in the New Testament alone, and that is more often than there are chapters from Matthew to Revelation (216)!

To let you really get a feel for the extensive scriptural coverage of this subject, and to acquaint you with the unique technique of this book in getting you ready to study prophecy for yourself, please get a pencil or pen and fill in the study guide on the next few pages after carefully examining the Scriptures listed. Don't try to look for some hidden meaning in each text, but simply answer the questions or write down the obvious meaning of the verse in the lines allotted.

| STUDY GUIDE 1 |

The Certainty of Christ's Second Coming

✦

Matthew 24. Describe Christ's second coming as depicted in—

verse 27: _____

_____

verse 30: _____

_____

Mark 13:27. What will Christ do when He comes? _____

_____

_____

Luke 21:25-28. What do you conclude from the fact He mentioned this coming in these three Gospels? _____

_____

_____

_____

John 14:1-3. What specific promise did our Lord make here? _____

_____

_____

Acts 1:10,11. Quote the angel's promise. _____

_____

_____

Philippians 3:20,21. Where will Christ come from and what will He do when He comes? _____

_____

_____

1 Thessalonians 3:13. How does God want us to be when Christ comes? _____

_____

_____

2 Thessalonians 2:1. What is the subject of this chapter?

_____

_____

James 5:8. How should we live until Christ returns? ___

_____

_____

Jude 14,15. List three things about the Lord's return. ___

_____

_____

_____

✦

The preceding Scriptures are only a few of the 318 references in the New Testament to the second coming of the Lord, but they will give you a feel for the fact that it is an extremely prominent subject in the biblical record. Christ's second coming is clearly mentioned or alluded to in 22 of the 27 New Testament books, and of the five books that make no clear mention of it, three of these (Philemon, 2 John, and 3 John) are short, one-chapter personal letters. Only two doctrinal books make no mention of the subject (Galatians and Romans), although Romans 11:26,27 contains a quotation from the Old Testament of the second coming of Messiah, so technically this book could be considered among those which contain a reference to the second coming.

SUMMARY

While there are many disagreements among Christians about the *time* of our Lord's coming, there is little disagreement over the fact that He *will* return. We have seen several of His specific promises to return again and take us to be with Himself, and since the Bible says, "His word cannot fail," we know it will happen. In addition, the angels promised He would return, as did His disciples many times. The apostle Paul is a good example, he mentioned the communion ordinance only twice in his 13 epistles and baptism only 13 times, but he mentioned the return of our Lord 50 times! It is one of the most frequently mentioned subjects in the Scripture, and a doctrinal necessity, for most Bible doctrines are so dependent upon it that they would not make much sense without it. It is the cornerstone of prophecy and, next to salvation, the most important doctrine in the Bible. Christ's second coming is the next major event of prophecy. As such, it is worthy of our detailed study.

The second coming is so much a part of Christianity that even many unsaved people with only a limited knowledge of Scripture believe He will return to this earth. This may indicate a yearning of many lost people who see the hopeless mess of world affairs. Somehow they yearn to see a benevolent leader come on the world scene to offer peace, prosperity, and health to a war-weary, poverty-stricken, and disease-ridden world. Only Jesus Christ qualifies to be that leader!

CHAPTER 4

Two Second Comings or One?

✦

We might as well deal right at the beginning with the *time* of Christ's coming, the most controversial aspect of our Lord's second coming. Few, if any, Christian scholars do not recognize the *fact* of His coming again to this earth. The main controversy surrounds the subject of *when* He will return and that includes whether He will come for His church (or all Christian believers) at one point in the future and then come for everyone else at a later date, or whether He will come for His church and all other believers at the same time.

It is imperative to point out here that fine Christians are to be found on almost all sides of this issue. It is also important to realize that while we can be dogmatic about such doctrines as the virgin birth, the deity of our Lord, the inerrancy of the Scriptures, the need to be born again, salvation by grace through faith, and certain other doctrines—including the fact of our Lord's second coming—this does not mean that we can be totally dogmatic about the *time* of His coming. The Bible gives many details associated with Christ's coming throughout the prophetic passages of Scripture, many of which have given rise to different interpretations in that the events involved are located at different times. We should develop a sense of respect for those who hold a position that is different from our own.

The purpose of this book is to help you study these prophetic passages for yourself, so you can come to a position that you can support from the Word of God. Then your beliefs will be based on personal study rather than on the teachings of another person. That is why it is important for you to fill in the questions asked in the study guides that follow *before* you try to make up your own mind or before you read my summary. It may be that you will not accept my summary or interpretation, and that's fine. All I ask is that you be persuaded by the Scriptures themselves and not by someone else's interpretation of them. That is particularly true of Figure 1 (p. 34), which conveys the idea that several second coming passages seem to contradict each other. I say *seem* to contradict because there are no real contradictions in the Bible. Let us first examine these seeming contradictions and then see if we can harmonize them.

STUDY GUIDE 2

The Two Contrasting Phases of Christ's Second Coming

✦

---

1 Thessalonians 4:17. In this text, locate where Christ will come. _____

_____

Matthew 25:31,32. Does this occur in heaven or in the air or on the earth? _____

_____

Revelation 19:15-19. When Christ comes as "King of Kings and Lord of Lords," where does He conquer the nations and judge the kings—in heaven or on earth? _____

_____

Zechariah 14:4,9: Tells specifically where He will come.

_____

Mark 13:33-37. This passage describes one aspect of His coming. Select one word based on verse 37 to describe it.

_____

Mark 13:26. Contrast that to this verse. _____

_____

_____

Matthew 24:30. This verse indicates the reaction of the people who see Christ at His coming. What is it? _____

_____

_____

✦

Now examine Figure 1 and see if it represents your findings.

These are only some of the contrasting views of Christ's coming in Scripture that must be harmonized. While some Bible teachers believe that the rapture and second coming per se happen simultaneously, many others believe that there are two different parts or phases of His one coming.

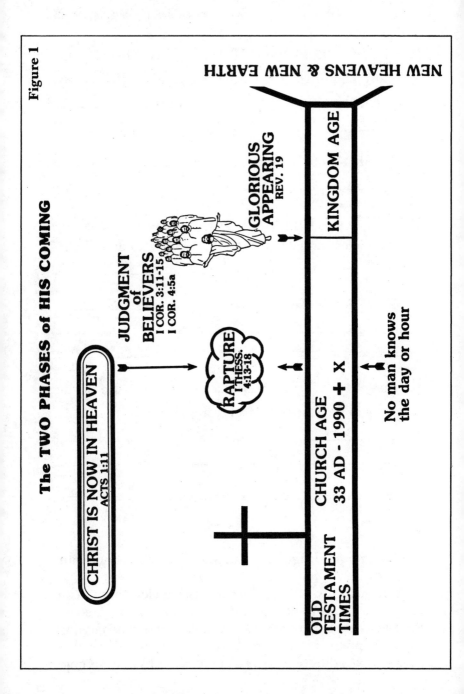

Figure 1

The TWO PHASES of HIS COMING

CHRIST IS NOW IN HEAVEN
ACTS 1:11

JUDGMENT of BELIEVERS
I COR. 3:11-15
I COR. 4:5a

GLORIOUS APPEARING
REV. 19

RAPTURE
I THESS. 4:13-18

NEW HEAVENS & NEW EARTH

KINGDOM AGE

OLD TESTAMENT TIMES

CHURCH AGE
33 AD - 1990 + X

No man knows the day or hour

For example, Christ is now in heaven, from which the angel promised He would come again to this earth. The first phase of His coming is "in the air" for believers; it will be secret and a great blessing to all who participate in it. This is called by Bible scholars "the rapture," based on the Greek word *harpazo* which means "to snatch away." The same word is used in Acts 8:39 and describes how the Holy Spirit "snatched away Philip" after he baptized the Ethiopian. Paul also used this word to describe his experience of being "caught up to the third heaven" (2 Corinthians 12:2-4). "Rapture" has come to mean the phase of our Lord's return in the air just for Christians, who are "caught up" together with the resurrected saints who have been "asleep in Jesus."

According to 1 Thessalonians 4:13-18, which is the most complete description of the "rapture" phase of Christ's coming, the rapture is preceded by the resurrection of all Christians who have died since the founding of Christianity. They are not really "dead," since their souls and spirits have been "absent from the body [at death] and present with the Lord." That is what is meant by "asleep in Jesus"—which goes on until the Lord comes. Only a few passages in the New Testament and none in the Old Testament describe this phase, which will be described in detail later. But because it is a time of reuniting both dead believers and those who are "alive and remain," plus the fact that they will all "meet the Lord in the air," it is a time of great blessing called "that blessed hope."

The second phase of the Lord's second coming is the public appearance of Christ to this earth, when He is accompanied with power and great glory as well as the angels of heaven. At that time He will set up His earthly kingdom. We call this "the glorious appearing of Christ." At that time "every eye shall see Him," and those who rejected Him will mourn because they will finally realize who He really is and that it is now too late to accept Him by faith as Lord and Savior. The overwhelming number of references to the second coming in both the Old and New Testaments have to do with this phase of our Lord's coming; only a few references describe His coming for His church, called the "rapture." Immediately after the rapture will come the "judgment seat of Christ" in the air (before He finishes His second coming with the second phase or glorious appearing). *These are not two comings of Christ but are two phases of His one coming.* The first phase is for Christians, and the second phase is for the world of unbelievers.

As you examine Figure 1 (p. 34) labeled "The Two Phases of Christ's Coming," you will find that the Lord leaves heaven only once, at the first phase of His coming "in the air" (the rapture), which we have seen is only for believers. Then, while still in the air, He conducts the judgment of believers. It is not well understood by Christians that all people will be judged, both believers and unbelievers. That is why we will dedicate a whole chapter to this subject. For now, however, I want you to note that the Lord remains "in the air," where He conducts this judgment of Christians and where their rewards (or lack of them) will be administered. (Believers will "rule and reign with Him" according to this judgment on the basis of what good works they performed after they became Christians.) Then, after an undisclosed period of time during which that judgment takes place, the Lord finishes His second coming by descending the rest of the way to the earth "in power and great glory, with the holy angels" to rule and reign literally during what the Scripture calls the kingdom age, which we shall also study in a future chapter.

The important fact to appreciate here is that it is all one coming. The two phases of His one second coming are in different places, at different times, for different people, and for different purposes. Some scholars believe it will all be done simultaneously. While this theory is held by many good people and solves some problems, it seems to this author that it creates far more than it solves. For one, it all but ignores the differences already pointed out. It makes no allowances for the judgment of believers—unless it is all done in an instant of time (which is possible, though not likely, since that would not allow for individual treatment and reward). In addition, this view leaves out several important events that will go on during that time.

THE RAPTURE PHASE

Now that you understand when the rapture phase of our Lord's second return occurs, let's examine those passages that deal primarily with the rapture. In the paragraph below I have reproduced the passage without comment from the New King James Version of the Bible, a highly regarded translation. These verses describe 18 steps or events in the rapture; please write them into the spaces provided for your own research in Study Guide 3.

> I do not want you to be ignorant, brethren, concerning those who have fallen asleep, lest you sorrow as others who have no hope. For if we believe that Jesus died and rose again, even so God will bring with Him those who sleep in Jesus. For this we say to you by the word of the Lord, that we who are alive and remain until the coming of the Lord will by no means precede those who are asleep. For the Lord Himself will descend from heaven with a shout, with the voice of an archangel, and with the trumpet of God. And the dead in Christ will rise first. Then we who are alive and remain shall be caught up together with them in the clouds to meet the Lord in the air. And thus we shall always be with the Lord. Therefore comfort one another with these words (1 Thessalonians 4:13-18).

The Rapture According to 1 Thessalonians 4:13-18

✦

Verse 13. What kind of people did Paul *not* want them to be? _____

_____

List his two purposes in giving this teaching.
1) _____
2) _____

To whom did Paul address this teaching? _____

Verse 14. Whom did he say Jesus would bring when He comes again? _____

_____

Verse 15. Where did Paul get this teaching? _____

_____

What is the event he is describing? _____

_____

Who will *not* precede dead believers? _____

_____

Verse 16. List the three things that happen when the Lord "descends from heaven."

1) _____

2) _____

3) _____

Who responds first? _____

Verse 17. List four things that happen in sequence.

1) _____

2) _____

3) _____

4) _____

Verse 18. Reread verse 13's last phrase and verse 18, and then describe why Paul wrote this passage. _____

_____

STUDY GUIDE 4

The Rapture According to 1 Corinthians 15:50-58

◆

The fifteenth chapter of 1 Corinthians is the great resurrection chapter of the Bible. Actually, the primary purpose of the Bible is about the coming resurrection of the dead. Only the Bible gives factual information about this event that can inspire believers. Note how closely this section of Scripture parallels the rapture passage. This passage describes more details about what happens when the rapture occurs, and should be studied along with 1 Thessalonians 4:16,17.

Verse 50. How does Paul describe the resurrected body?

_____

_____

Verse 51. List two parts of this "mystery" which Paul reveals.

1) _____
2) _____

Verse 52. How fast will this change occur? _____

_____

What does the trumpet signal? _____

_____

Verses 53-57. How essential is this change into the incorruptible? _____

_____

What victory does Christ give us? _____

_____

_____

Verse 58. What conclusion does Paul draw from this teaching on resurrection at the rapture? _____

_____

Why? _____

_____

STUDY GUIDE 5

Jesus' Only Direct Reference to the Rapture

✦

Our Lord referred directly to the rapture only once (John 14:1-3). All His other teachings on His coming have to do with the second phase because it refers to the literal, physical return when He will set up His kingdom, for which the Jews (to whom He spoke) were looking. However, the day before He died on the cross He was preparing His disciples to function during His absence (the church age) and addressed them with these words:

> Let not your heart be troubled; you believe in God, believe also in Me. In My Father's house are many mansions; if it were not so, I would have told you. I go to prepare a place for you. And if I go and prepare a place for you, I will come again and receive you to Myself, that where I am, there you may be also (John 14:1-3).

Describe what He was saying. Specifically identify the phase of His coming that He had in mind. _____

_____

Where have the disciples lived (in their present soulish state) since their death until now?

14:1 _____

14:3c _____

Note: Why do you think these three passages are the most frequent Bible passages used at funerals or burial services of Christians?

_____

_____

_____

✦

THE PUBLIC, VISIBLE PHASE OF HIS COMING

We have already seen that the second phase of our Lord's coming, which we call *the glorious appearing*, is the one most frequently mentioned in the Scriptures, both in the Old and New Testaments. It is the event which all the prophets of Israel looked forward to and is the one which the disciples had in mind when they asked our Lord, "What will be THE sign of Your coming, and of the end of the age?" (Matthew 24:3). We shall study this in detail in a later chapter, but here I just call your attention to the way the disciples identified "the coming of the Lord" and "the end of the age." When Christ comes physically to this earth, it will be to end this period of time and usher in a whole new age—not the pantheistic mysticism of the New Age movement, but a whole new age for mankind when God Himself will be their King of Kings and will rule over them. As we shall see, it will fulfill the fondest dreams of all those who humble themselves before God.

For a complete description of that event, read both our Lord's prophecy of it in Matthew 24:29-31 and 25:31-46 and the apostle John's account in Revelation 19:11-21. Then examine Daniel the prophet, who in the second chapter of his book described four successive world governments. Then he predicted in verse 44 their destruction and replacement by an everlasting kingdom established by God. The only hint I will give you now is about "the rock cut without hands" in the king's vision, which will destroy all the other kingdoms and fill the whole earth (see Daniel 2:35). Christ, of course, is the "rock of ages" (1 Corinthians 10:4).

STUDY GUIDE 6

The Glorious Appearing

✦

On the lines below, briefly summarize what these passages teach about the glorious appearing phase of our Lord's second coming.

Matthew 24:29-31. _____

_____

_____

_____

_____

Matthew 25:31-46. _____

_____

_____

_____

_____

Revelation 19:11-21. _____

_____

_____

_____

_____

Daniel 2:35-44. _____

_____

_____

_____

_____

◆

CHAPTER 5

The Tribulation That Separates the Phases

✦

Now we come to a very important part of our second coming studies: the events that occur between the rapture phase and the public phase of Christ's return. We have already mentioned that our Lord will judge His church "in the air" before He finishes His coming physically to the earth to set up His kingdom, and we will explore this in detail in a later chapter. But so far we have not mentioned anything about what takes place here on the earth during that time. To find the answer to that question, we will have to study our Lord's very definitive Olivet Discourse, which I have reserved for a later chapter. However, the great Old Testament prophets, particularly Daniel, had much to say about that time period, and the book of Revelation uses 13 chapters to describe it in detail.

In short, that space of time is called by prophecy students:

THE TRIBULATION PERIOD

Anyone who takes the Bible literally must face the fact that it teaches there is a time of *tribulation* awaiting the inhabitants of this earth (some translations refer to it as "great distress"). Our Lord said of it, "There will be great distress, unequaled from the beginning of the world until now" (Matthew 24:21 NIV). As we will see, the conditions which the Bible describes for this tribulation time have never occurred up to this time in all of world history. This tribulation period, which occupies so much space in Scripture, must be located somewhere in the future. And because of its prominence in the Bible, locating it has generated no small amount of controversy. As a general rule of thumb, the more literally a person takes the prophetic portions of Scripture, the more prone he is to believe that the tribulation is a literal time of future trauma when the Antichrist (a real person) will rule the world. You will find a study of life on this earth during that period both interesting and traumatic. The main point of controversy is whether the church will go through this period or will be raptured before it begins.

The time of the tribulation period is generally considered to be seven years, based on Daniel's prophetic vision of 9:24-27. In this vision the prophet was told that "70 weeks" (or 70 "heptads," meaning 70 times 7 weeks of years, for a total of 490 years) were "determined for your people [the Jews] and the Holy City." He then lists three periods of time, beginning with "seven weeks [or 49 years] from the going forth of the command to restore and rebuild Jerusalem" (which is described in the book of Ezra and Nehemiah as the time when the walls and the temple were rebuilt). The second period was "62 weeks" (or 434 years) until "Messiah shall be cut off, but not for Himself." (This is an obvious reference to the period from the rededication of the temple to the crucifixion of Jesus the Messiah.) That leaves one heptad (seven-year period) of tribulation for the Jews that has never been fulfilled. This is usually called the "time of Jacob's trouble," as described in Jeremiah 30:3-11. It is also described by our Lord in the Olivet Discourse and in the book of Revelation, where it is called "the tribulation." Study Figure 2 carefully.

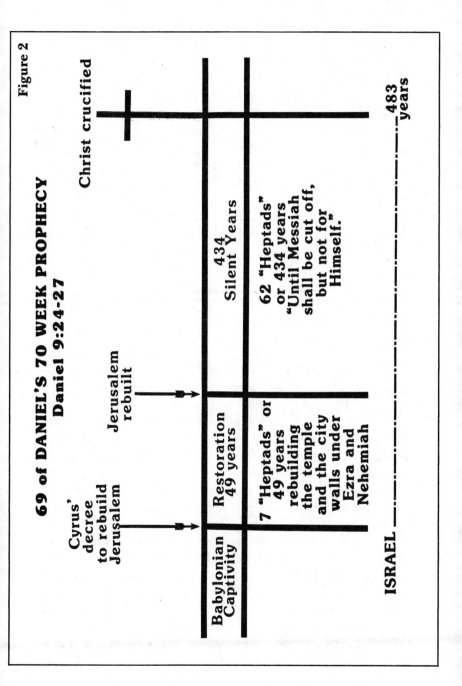

Figure 2

69 of DANIEL'S 70 WEEK PROPHECY
Daniel 9:24-27

Cyrus' decree to rebuild Jerusalem

Jerusalem rebuilt

Christ crucified

| Babylonian Captivity | Restoration 49 years | 434 Silent Years | |

7 "Heptads" or 49 years rebuilding the temple and the city walls under Ezra and Nehemiah

62 "Heptads" or 434 years "Until Messiah shall be cut off, but not for Himself."

ISRAEL ———————————— 483 years

Only 69 heptads (weeks of years) have been fulfilled so far. One heptad of seven years has never been fulfilled. The church age began immediately after the descent of the Holy Spirit on the day of Pentecost, and therefore the remaining period "determined" for Israel is yet future. Keep in mind that this prophecy of Daniel is about *Israel*; it was not given to or about the church. It was given about what would happen to the Jews, and therefore no mention is made of the church. Notice instead that Daniel 9:26b points out that "the prince who is to come" (which can only be the Antichrist) will be a Roman, for it says that his people (the Romans of 70 A.D.) "shall destroy the city and the sanctuary."

So in the midst of talking about the rebuilding of the temple and the Holy City (during 49 years), Daniel predicted that it would be used for 434 years, then "Messiah shall be cut off." From Isaiah 53 we see that this was prophesied as the crucifixion which was described in the Gospels. Then after an unspecified period the temple would be destroyed. Historically that took 40 years. After another undesignated period of time (the church age, which really began at Pentecost and has gone on now for over 1900 years) there would be a period in which "there will be war; desolations are determined." A quick glance at these 1900-plus years of church history will reveal that it has been a continuous series of wars, from the Caesars to the Saracens, from the Turks to the Mongols, from the Crusades to the wars and revolutions of the Western world.

Then Daniel 9:27 says, "Then he [the prince that shall come] shall confirm a covenant with many for *one week*, but in the middle of the week he shall bring an end to sacrifice and offering." This is obviously a future event, and because it parallels prophetic teachings in 2 Thessalonians 2 and the book of Revelation, most prophecy teachers believe that the Antichrist will be the one to officially begin the tribulation period by signing a covenant with Israel for seven years (that unfulfilled seven years of Daniel). He will then break that covenant in 3^1/$_2$ years (or 42 months, as Revelation 13 describes it), after which the end (the "consummation") comes: the physical return of Christ to this earth to set up His ultimate kingdom. A study of Figure 3 will make this clear.*

* This chart is reproduced from Tim LaHaye, *Revelation Illustrated and Made Plain* (Grand Rapids: Zondervan, 1973, 1975), p. 93.

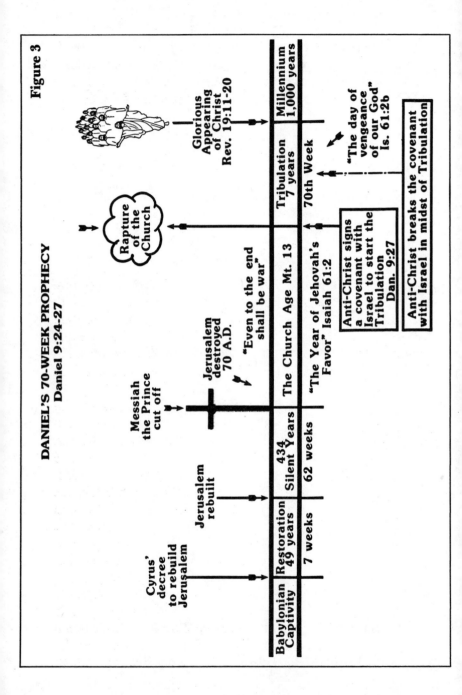

Figure 3

DANIEL'S 70-WEEK PROPHECY
Daniel 9:24-27

Cyrus' decree to rebuild Jerusalem

Jerusalem rebuilt

Messiah the Prince cut off

Jerusalem destroyed 70 A.D.

"Even to the end shall be war"

Rapture of the Church

Glorious Appearing of Christ Rev. 19:11-20

Babylonian Captivity	Restoration 49 years	Silent Years 434 Years	The Church Age Mt. 13	Tribulation 7 years	Millennium 1,000 years
	7 weeks	62 weeks		70th Week	

"The Year of Jehovah's Favor" Isaiah 61:2

"The day of vengeance of our God" Is. 61:2b

Anti-Christ signs a covenant with Israel to start the Tribulation Dan. 9:27

Anti-Christ breaks the covenant with Israel in midst of Tribulation

CHAPTER 6

Tribulation, the Heart of the Revelation

◆

The best way to decide whether the seven-year tribulation period is yet future is to examine the events forecast to happen during that time. And the best place to analyze those events is the book of Revelation, because more details are given there about that period than in any other place in the Bible, including our Lord's extensive reference to it in Matthew 24.

Keep in mind as you read that chapters 6 and 7 of Revelation go together and cover the first quarter of the tribulation. Chapters 8 and 9 then cover the second quarter. Chapter 11 culminates at that halfway point and chapter 13 begins there and runs simultaneously with chapter 16. While there are other subjects addressed in the book, the three sets of judgments described in chapters 6-7, 8-9, and in 16 are chronological and go together with the other two chapters I have cited. These will provide you ample evidence to see for yourself if these prophecies have been fulfilled in history or are events that are yet future.

It is very important that you complete the next study guide so that you can see for yourself how simple it is to understand the book of Revelation if you let the Bible mean what it says. (Some of chapter 9 refers to activities in the spirit world that seem to have a physical affect on human beings.) By reading chapters 6-16 and answering the following questions as you read, you should be able to discern for yourself these important events.

STUDY GUIDE 7

The Seal Judgments of the Tribulation

✦

Revelation 6 and 7

The first four seal judgments are the four horsemen. What effect do they have on the earth after they appear?

1) 6:1,2. _____

2) 6:3,4. _____

3) 6:5,6. _____

4) 6:7,8. _____

Describe briefly what the fifth seal reveals in verses 9-11.

_____

_____

_____

Read verses 12-16 and summarize the events. _____

_____

_____

What is the period of time called (verse 17)? _____

_____

_____

═══

| STUDY GUIDE 8 |

The 144,000 Witnesses
Revelation 7

✦

═══

Revelation 7:1-17. What are these people called (verse 3b)? _____

Who are they (verses 4-8)? _____

Describe the great multitude mentioned in verses 9-14.

_____

_____

Note verse 14. Who are these people? _____

_____

What is their reward (verses 15-17)? _____

_____

═══

✦

The seventh seal introduces the seven trumpet judgments, which is why many prophecy students consider these judgments to be chronological: The first six seals cover 21 months, then the breaking of the seventh seal introduces the next seven trumpet judgments, which describe events during the second quarter or the second 21 months. The sealing of the 144,000 "servants of our God" probably occurs at the beginning, and they witness all during this period, along with the special two witnesses described in Revelation chapter 11. But first we should examine the trumpet judgments.

STUDY GUIDE 9

The Trumpet Judgments
Revelation 8 and 9

✦

Describe the events on earth as a result of the first trumpet (8:6,7). _____

_____

The second (verses 8,9). _____

_____

The third (verses 10,11). _____

_____

The fourth (verse 12). _____

_____

The fifth (9:1-11). _____

_____

The sixth (verses 12-19). _____

_____

Note how the majority of people responded (verse 20a).

_____

List the six major sins of people during those days (verses 20,21).

1) _____

2) _____

3) _____

4) _____

5) _____

6) _____

✦

THE TWO WITNESSES

God never leaves mankind without adequate witness. During the first half of the tribulation period He not only has the 144,000 Israelites from each of the 12 tribes who reach "a multitude which no one can number," but He also establishes in and around Jerusalem two special witnesses endowed with supernatural powers (similar to two men in the Old Testament). It is important that you know what they do and what happens to them.

You probably noticed the two powerful forces that are simultaneously active during that time: 1) a mighty soul harvest under the witnessing of the 144,000 servants of God, and 2) the enormous sinfulness of those who refuse to repent. It is the same as in our own day—the church as it witnesses for her Lord on the one hand, and those who reject the Savior on the other, except that everything will be intensified during the tribulation period.

However, because the civil government described in Revelation 13 will be under the total control of the Antichrist and his evil forces, Christians will be persecuted and martyred until few (if any) will be left to go into the last half of the tribulation.

| STUDY GUIDE 10 |

God's Two Supernatural Witnesses
Revelation 11

✦

What important structure will be in existence that is not now (11:1)? _____

_____

Who will control the city of Jerusalem at that time? _____

_____

Describe the two witnesses. _____

_____

_____

How long will their ministry last (verse 3)? _____

Describe what happens to them after they finish their ministry (verse 7-10). _____

Note how these evil people hated them (verses 9,10).

What means of communication is necessary to fulfill verse 9?

_____

Could that have been possible before the present generation? _____

_____

Then what happens to them? _____

_____

Many Christians believe that these men were Old Testament characters because the things they will do are so similar to what the Old Testament personages did when they were on the earth. What two Old Testament men do they remind you of? _____

_____

✦

THE ANTICHRIST

Whenever the Bible uses a "beast" symbolically (which is quite obvious by its description—seven heads, ten horns, and a mouth speaking blasphemy), it always means *government*. An example is found in the prophecy of Daniel chapters 7 and 8. Most governments are repressive and persecute the common people; they usually hate God and try to keep the people from worshiping Him. The caesars and the past Communist dictators are obvious examples of this. The "beast" pictured in Revelation 13 is obviously the head of the coming world government because he so definitely takes on the functions of a person. In fact, he is joined in this chapter by a "false prophet" who is also human. We will study him from other passages, but it is important to know from this chapter some of what he will do when he assumes power. He will operate during all seven years of the tribulation, but this chapter deals primarily with the last half, when he will have almost total control of the people living on the earth at that time, which is why our Lord referred to the second half as "the great tribulation."

STUDY GUIDE 11

The Beast of Revelation 13

✦

Read the entire chapter.

The "dragon" in Scripture refers to the Devil. What three things will he give the Beast in verse 2?

1) _____

2) _____

3) _____

What kind of following will he have (verse 3c)? _____

_____

Who will be their object of worship? _____

How will he use his mouth (verses 5,6)? _____

How long will he have this total control (verse 5b)? _____

Name the three objects of his blasphemy (verse 6). _____

_____

What does verse 7a suggest to you? _____

_____

Does it seem that during this second 42 months there will be the worldwide evangelism of the first 42 months? _____

Then what will happen (verses 7,8)? _____

Who are the only ones who do not "worship the Beast" (verse 8)? _____

_____

Who are these people? To answer that question you should also read Philippians 4:3 and Revelation 3:5. _____

_____

What is God's challenge to the saints living during these days? _____

_____

In summarizing these events in verses 1-10, who is the Antichrist's (beast's) war against, and who will suffer? __

_____

_____

==

STUDY GUIDE 12

The False Prophet of Revelation 13

✦

==

Whenever a political leader tries to exterminate religion or the true worship of God, he must use the services of a false religious leader. The Antichrist will be no different. His leader will look "like a lamb" and speak "like a dragon" (verse 11). What does that suggest to you? _____

_____

_____

Where will he get his power (verse 12)? _____

What will he do with it? _____

_____

What other powers will he have (verse 13)? _____

_____

What effect will that have (verse 14a)? _____

_____

Describe the image (verses 14b-15). _____

_____

Describe the mark of the Beast (verses 16,17). _____

_____

What effect will it have on the economy? _____

_____

Six is the biblical number of man. What significance do you attach to the number of verse 18? _____

_____

_____

Summarize what life will be like for both the saved and unsaved living on the earth at this time, as described in Revelation 13. _____

_____

_____

If you take these events to be literal happenings, is there any possible way they could refer to anything that has ever before occurred in world history? _____

Note: More details of that last 42 months of the tribulation period are described in Revelation 16. Keep in mind that the events which these bowl judgments describe will occur during the time that the Antichrist rules the world, with the false prophet as his religious leader.

STUDY GUIDE 13

The Bowl Judgments of Revelation 16

✦

Each of the bowls, when poured out, creates a condition on the earth. In the spaces below, describe what happens on earth and note the reaction of mankind.

First bowl (verse 2): _____

_____

Reaction: _____

_____

Second bowl (verse 3): _____

_____

Reaction: _____

Third bowl (verse 4): _____

_____

Reaction: _____

Fourth bowl (verses 8,9): _____

_____

Reaction: _____

Fifth bowl (verses 10,11): _____

_____

Reaction: _____

Sixth bowl (verses 12-16): _____

_____

Reaction: _____

What famous future war is mentioned here (verses 14c,16c)?

_____

Verse 15 is parenthetical. Could this indicate that even at this late date in the tribulation period there will still be saints on the earth? _____

_____

Seventh bowl (verses 17-21): _____

_____

Reaction: _____

_____

This greatest earthquake that has ever taken place will occur at the same time as the events in Revelation 18, when God will destroy Babylon, the governmental and financial capital of the world. Chapter 17 occurs in the middle of the tribulation, when the kings of the earth destroy the religions of the world so that the worship of Antichrist can become the world religion.

In reality the seventh bowl judgment concludes the tribulation period. Revelation 19 reveals the next chronological event after the tribulation, which is the physical return of Christ to this earth in what the Scriptures call "the second coming." Christ then sets up His kingdom, which we will study later. But read how He disposes of the Antichrist and the false prophet at His coming.

Describe it (19:20). _____

_____

God's justification for what He will do to those who reject Him is given in Revelation 16:5-7. What does this passage teach that the godless will do during this period? _____

_____

On the chart below, draw your own time line describing the tribulation from your study, before you examine Figure 4 (shown later in this chapter).

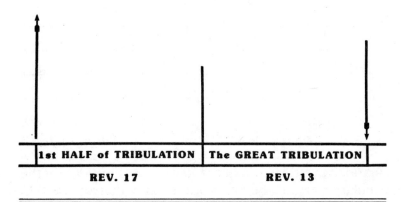

1st HALF of TRIBULATION	The GREAT TRIBULATION
REV. 17	REV. 13

✦

THREE IMPORTANT QUESTIONS

In looking over these events which will happen during the tribulation, ask yourself the important question again, Has such a series of events ever yet occurred in a seven-year period of history? The answer is a resounding *no!* In fact, none of these events has ever occurred even *singly* during the entire 1900-year history of the church, nor have two men ever been on this earth like the Antichrist and the False Prophet. The reason this fact is important is that it will help you locate the sequence of the rapture and the physical coming of Christ to the earth. (More on this in a later chapter.)

However, there is still one extremely important question that you should ask yourself here. You probably noticed that there are only two kinds of people on the earth during the tribulation period: those who accept Christ by faith in His blood shed on the cross for their sins, and those who reject Him and instead follow the Antichrist (and who end up killing those who believe and blaspheme the name of God). Although the conditions right now are much different, since we do not have a one-world autocratic ruler yet, there are still just two kinds of people: those who have accepted Jesus by faith and those who have not. My question is, Where do you stand? As we close this chapter, it would be a good exercise for you to answer the following two questions.

Have you ever personally invited Christ to come into your life to forgive your sin and save your soul? _____

If so, when? _____

If you haven't done so or are not sure you have, may I suggest that you do so right now? To have your name written in the Lamb's book of life, you must be one of His. And you are either one of His or one of this world's. But you may say, "I'm in-between. I haven't accepted Him, but I don't want to follow the Antichrist either." What you don't understand is that there is really no middle ground. Our Lord said, "He that is not with me is against me." And after what we have studied, I'm sure you don't want to be against Him. So right now while you're reading this book you can call on the name of the Lord by faith and be saved. A simple prayer of faith often goes something like this: "Dear Lord, I have sinned against You and Your law. I believe that Your Son, Jesus, died for my sin on the cross and rose on the third day from the grave. Please come into my life and forgive my sin. I give myself to You." If you have not prayed a simple yet sincere prayer like this, please do so and enter your name and today's date in the space below.

Name _____ Date _____

Then tell someone about your decision and see what has happened to you according to Romans 10:9,10. I would also like to know of your decision.

SUMMARY

If you take these chapters in Revelation literally, you are forced to come to the conclusion that no such tribulation period has ever before occurred in history. True, this world has known tribulation, trials, famines, earthquakes, and pestilences, but never have events like *these* occurred. There are countries of the world where Christians have been martyred by the thousands. In fact many Christians living during the fifteenth and sixteenth centuries, as well as those living in Communist countries during the twentieth century, thought they were in the biblical tribulation. But even though they were in severe tribulation in a general sense, they were not in "the great tribulation." At no time, so far in world history, have all the events we have just studied in Revelation been fulfilled.

WHAT BEGINS THE
TRIBULATION PERIOD?

The prophecy of Daniel 9:27 tells us exactly what will start the tribulation period: when "he [the prince that shall come] shall confirm a covenant with many of one week." It seems that the Antichrist will make a covenant with Daniel's people for seven years. That may be what is meant by the rider on the white horse of Revelation 6 who comes in peace, for he has no arrows or implements of war in his hand. Instead, by offering peace to the world he will make a covenant with Israel, and the Jewish people will have peace in the Holy Land, will rebuild their temple, and will reinstate their sacrifices again—for $3^1/_2$ years! But "in the middle of the week [of years, or after $3^1/_2$ years has elapsed] he shall bring an end to sacrifice and offering. And on the wing of abominations shall be one who makes desolate (Daniel 9:27). Antichrist will break his covenant with the Jews in the middle of the tribulation (which agrees with Revelation 11 and 13) and will launch the greatest time of desolation in the history of the world. How long will it last? "Until the consummation, which is determined." This is the same as "the time of the end," meaning the end of the 70 weeks or 490 years, which is the same as the "consummation" of God's dealing with the Jews and the literal coming of Christ to set up His kingdom.

What is important to see here is that the tribulation period is begun by the signing of a covenant of peace between the coming new world government headed by the Antichrist and the nations of the world, including Israel. But when he gains total control, after $3^1/_2$ years, he breaks that covenant and begins to persecute the nation of Israel, and they become "desolate."

Many Christians think that the rapture of the church begins the tribulation period, but while the rapture and the signing of the covenant may take place very close together, the Bible is not specific on that subject. I have read suggestions that the two events may occur anywhere from 50 years apart to the same day. (More on this in a later chapter.)

The point here is that there has never been a "man of sin" or Antichrist-type world ruler who has made a covenant of peace with many nations, including Israel, for seven years, and then broken that covenant with Israel at the halfway point. This obviously means that such events are yet future.

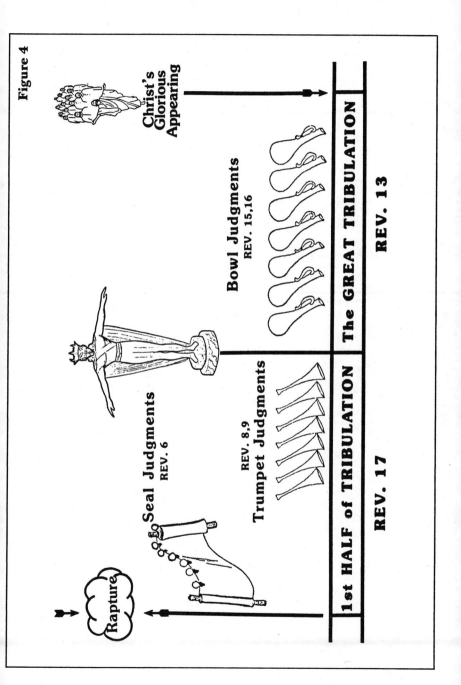

Figure 4

CHAPTER 7

Rapture Before Tribulation?

✦

Will the rapture of the church occur before the tribulation period begins? This is a question that has generated more than its share of heat and not enough light from the Scriptures. Many Christians differ on this subject, which indicates that while Scripture is very clear on the *fact* that Christ will come again, it is not as clear on whether He will come for His church before, in the middle of, or at the end of the tribulation.

There are several Scriptures that are used by Christians to support either view. You should know your own view and be prepared to defend it, but you should not be dogmatic to the point of breaking fellowship with anyone who does not agree with you. Figure 5 and a brief synopsis of each view should be studied carefully.

VIEWS OF WHEN THE RAPTURE OCCURS

The *pretribulation view* teaches that Christ will come in the air, resurrect the dead in Christ of the church age (1 Thessalonians 4:16,17 and 1 Corinthians 15:50-56), and rapture His church up to be with Him before the tribulation period begins, thus saving them from "the day of wrath

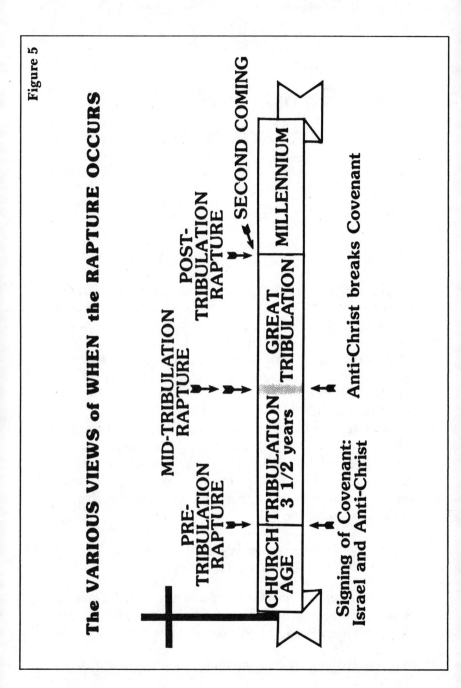

Figure 5

The VARIOUS VIEWS of WHEN the RAPTURE OCCURS

PRE-TRIBULATION RAPTURE

MID-TRIBULATION RAPTURE

POST-TRIBULATION RAPTURE

SECOND COMING

CHURCH AGE

TRIBULATION 3 1/2 years

GREAT TRIBULATION

MILLENNIUM

Signing of Covenant: Israel and Anti-Christ

Anti-Christ breaks Covenant

that shall try the whole earth." The world will then go through seven years of tribulation, and then Christ will finish His coming by descending in power and great glory to the earth to set up His millennial kingdom.

The *midtribulation view* teaches that the church will go through the first half of the tribulation period, and that Christ will come in the air to rapture His church and resurrect the dead in Christ (1 Thessalonians 4:16,17 and 1 Corinthians 15:50-56) in the middle of the seven years, prior to the great tribulation period of 3½ more years. Then Christ comes in glory to set up His kingdom.

The *posttribulation view* teaches that the church will go through the entire tribulation period, that many church saints will be martyred, and that the Lord will resurrect dead believers up to that point and rapture those who are alive at the time by catching them up to Him as He descends, and then finish His coming to the earth in power to set up His kingdom.

You will note several similarities between these views: the resurrection of the dead, the catching up or rapture of those alive at the time, and the literal coming of Christ to the earth. Even some posttribulationists believe there will be a brief time lapse between the rapture and the "glorious appearing" or second coming of Christ to the earth.

The main difference is timing: *When* will Christ resurrect the dead saints and rapture His church? While there are slight variations within each of the above belief systems, these three views represent the prevailing views of most Christians who believe that Christ will come prior to the millennial kingdom. It is good to keep in mind that the major difference is determined by whether you take the prophecies about the tribulation literally or metaphorically. Since similar tragic events have already happened before in the Old Testament (either in the plagues of Egypt or the judgments of God on Israel and the pagan nations), there is no real reason to reject the idea that the prophesied events should be taken literally and will happen exactly as predicted.

CHAPTER 8

The Church Is Distinct from Israel

✦

Before we go further we should point out that the church is not Israel and Israel is not the church. Some of the most confusing prophetic voices today teach that there is no distinction between Israel and the church, and that the church today is spiritual Israel and is destined to fulfill the promises of God to that chosen nation.

But in so doing these teachers overlook the very important fact that Jesus Christ promised during the time of Israel (in fact just about a year before the end of the 69th week of years promised to Daniel when He would "be cut off" on the cross) that *He* would "build My church, and the gates of Hades shall not prevail against it" (Matthew 16:18).

This is not to imply that the church is better than Israel, but simply that it is *different*. During "the acceptable year of the Lord" (Luke 4:19), the preaching of the gospel would be the way into Christ's church. He even promised to give Peter "the keys to the kingdom of heaven," which Peter used when he was the first person to preach the gospel to the Jews on the day of Pentecost. Peter used the second key in Acts 10, when he was the first Christian to preach the gospel to the Gentiles.

For a clear understanding of the church, please complete the Bible study of Ephesians 3:1-12 provided on the next page. You should understand that when the New Testament talks about a "mystery" it is not referring to some mysterious teaching that cannot be understood; instead, it is talking about something that was not known in Old Testament times but is revealed to us in the New Testament.

STADY GUIDE 14

The Mystery of the Church Revealed
Ephesians 3:1-12

✦

What was given to Paul in Ephesians 3:2? _____

How did he learn this "mystery"? _____

What does that suggest to you? _____

_____

Is it possible to understand this "mystery"? _____
How? _____

Why didn't Israel, in the Old Testament, understand this (verse 5)? _____

_____

How is it made known today (verse 5)? _____

_____

What then is one of the purposes of the church age (verse 6)? _____

_____

Would you say that "the church," meaning the whole body of Christ made up of believers of all the ages, is made up primarily of Jews or of Gentiles? _____

Now do you see why the church is often referred to as the period of time when God works primarily with Gentiles?

_____

What is the church's commission (verse 10)? _____

_____

What does verse 11 mean? _____

_____

What is the result (verse 12)? _____

_____

Did the Jews in the days when God was working with Israel have this same access? _____

The reason is that Christ had not yet died for the sins of the world.

✦

ISRAEL IS NOT THE CHURCH

God worked primarily through Israel in the Old Testament, but God revealed to Daniel the prophet that 490 years would "be determined" until Messiah was cut off. Then an undetermined period of time would transpire which Isaiah called "the year of God's favor." Our Lord, just before He died on the cross "for the sins of the whole world," began His church, which would be His primary lighthouse for proclaiming the gospel during that period of time we call "the church age," which has been going on now for over 1900 years. However, in the end times which God told Daniel about in 12:1 (and also other prophets) He would fulfill the many other prophecies to Israel that have not yet been fulfilled, culminating in the second coming of Messiah to set up His kingdom. Before that event, however, the unfulfilled "week" of Daniel (that is, seven years) would be fulfilled. That is what Jesus addressed in His Olivet Discourse, which we shall study later. These distinct periods of time are identified in Figure 6.

It is important to understand that God has now (since the finished work of Christ on the cross) changed His dealing with man. Salvation is no longer accomplished by having faith in the blood sacrifice of animals, as in the Old Testament. Now, in the new economy of God's grace to man (which the book of Hebrews tells us repeatedly is "far better"), men can be saved by faith in Jesus Christ when they voluntarily turn their lives over to Him as Lord and Savior (Romans 10:9,10).

This monumental event, when "Messiah shall be cut off, but not for Himself" (which we call the crucifixion), introduced a whole new age or period of time: "the acceptable year [period of time] of the Lord's favor." And then shall come the last of Isaiah's prophecy, "the day of vengeance of our God." God has designed the traumatic events of the tribulation period to get a maximum number of people to

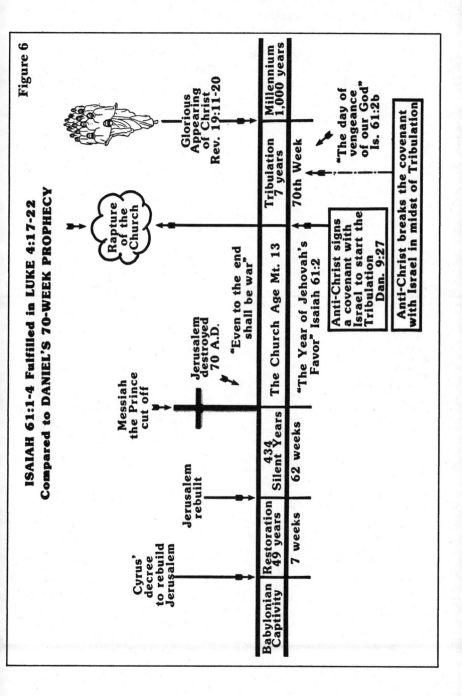

Figure 6

ISAIAH 61:1-4 Fulfilled in LUKE 4:17-22
Compared to DANIEL'S 70-WEEK PROPHECY

Glorious Appearing of Christ Rev. 19:11-20

Millennium 1,000 years

Tribulation 7 years

70th Week

"The day of vengeance of our God" Is. 61:2b

Anti-Christ breaks the covenant with Israel in midst of Tribulation

Anti-Christ signs a covenant with Israel to start the Tribulation Dan. 9:27

Rapture of the Church

The Church Age Mt. 13

"The Year of Jehovah's Favor" Isaiah 61:2

Jerusalem destroyed 70 A.D.

"Even to the end shall be war"

Messiah the Prince cut off

434 Silent Years

62 weeks

Jerusalem rebuilt

Restoration 49 years

7 weeks

Cyrus' decree to rebuild Jerusalem

Babylonian Captivity

come to faith in His Son. While this time may seem cruel to some, it is actually an act of mercy on the part of God, since it will result in millions of people turning to Him in faith, thereby saving their immortal souls.

CHAPTER 9

Christians Will Be Saved from the Wrath

◆

Not only does "the acceptable year of the Lord's favor" (the church age) come to a distinct end, to be followed by the "day of God's wrath" (the unfulfilled period of seven years), but God has given His church ample evidence in Scripture that it will not go through that tribulation period. The reason is not that Christians deserve to be spared from it, since we don't deserve any of the blessings that God has bestowed upon us. The true reason is that *the tribulation period is not for the church.* Instead, it is for Israel to fulfill prophecy, and for the Gentiles to be judged if they refuse to repent. Anyone who fails to distinguish between the church, Israel, and the Gentile world will have a difficult time understanding most of prophecy. Paul makes that distinction quite clear in 1 Corinthians 10:32, where he writes, "Give no offense, either to the Jews or to the Greeks or to the church of God."

The church is really made up of both Jews and Gentiles ("Greeks") who have spiritually experienced the "born-again" relationship with Him by faith. They have entered into His kingdom spiritually by faith, awaiting the day when they will enter His physical kingdom by His glory and power at His second coming. They are not appointed to wrath (or the period of wrath), which is really for unbelieving Jews and Gentiles.

Our Lord in His Olivet Discourse alluded to the Christians' escape from the coming day of wrath that shall try the whole earth: "Watch therefore, and pray always that you may be counted worthy to escape all these things that will come to pass, and to stand before the Son of Man" (Luke 21:36).

In 1 Thessalonians 5:9, after talking about "the times and seasons" and "the day of the Lord," Paul said, "For God has not appointed us to wrath, but to obtain salvation through our Lord Jesus Christ." This is an obvious reference to the "day of wrath" which we saw so vividly described in Revelation 6, which in verse 17 says, "The great day of His wrath has come, and who is able to stand?" This confirms the fact that the church is not appointed to wrath but to salvation or deliverance. (Some prophecy teachers associate this wrath with the final judgment and hell, which Christians are of course exempt from also, but the context of this wrath is not hell but the tribulation period.)

We see the same thing in 1 Thessalonians 1:9,10, where we find that Christ at His coming will "deliver us from the wrath to come." This is similar to the challenge which the Spirit of God gave to the church of Philadelphia (which many interpreters think represents the Bible-believing church of our own day): "Because you have kept My command to persevere, I also will keep you from the hour of trial which shall come upon all the world, to test those who dwell on the earth" (Revelation 3:10). Notice that our Lord promised those believers they would be "kept *from the hour of trial* which shall come upon all the world," and not merely kept while they go through it.

Some Bible teachers (among whom are some of my personal friends) think it weakens the church to teach that we are such Pollyanna Christians that we have to be saved from the tribulation wrath, and that if we are wrong in our pretribulation view, this will create tragic disillusionment among believers when they find themselves in the tribulation period. Frankly, I have more confidence in Christians than that. If we are wrong about this interpretation and wake up in the first or second half of the tribulation, I am confident that with God's help we will be able to take it.

But if we had to look forward to going through the biblically described tribulation before Christ comes, it would be difficult for any of us to look forward to it with any degree of expectation. Can you imagine challenging Christians to look forward to the coming of Christ and then adding, "Oh, by the way, before He comes you must suffer the horrors of the tribulation period"!

Looking forward to such tribulation events before the coming of Christ for believers is hardly "the blessed hope" that Paul challenges Christians to look forward to. Furthermore, if the Lord comes for His church *after* the tribulation, it cannot be "unexpected" the way a "thief comes," for the physical coming of Christ to the earth will not be secret or unexpected. If the posttribulationist view is right, Christ will come exactly seven years from the time the Antichrist signs the covenant with Israel, or as Revelation 13 states it, two periods of 42 months. What would be secret about that?

The secret rapture phase of Christ's coming for His church will be *sudden and unexpected*. Except for those who "look for Him" and are "ready at His coming" (in other words, are spiritually prepared for Him), His coming will catch people unprepared. Christians who live worldly, carnal lives show by their deeds that they have little anticipation for His coming.

Fortunately, we are all going up in the rapture at the same time, suddenly and unexpectedly when He calls—not when we *think* He is coming. As one of my midtribulationist friends says, He will not "shout from heaven" just to those who are pretribulation rapturists, with the idea that He will stage another rapture for those who expect Him in the middle of the tribulation and a third for the posttribulationists. Instead, when He comes we are all going up at the same time!

There is another passage that contains a specific reference to our being taken out before the tribulation comes, and that passage is 2 Thessalonians 2:3. I have not used it until now because the Old King James rendering of this verse has created much unnecessary confusion: "Let no man deceive you by any means; for that day shall not come except there come *a falling away first*, and that man of sin be revealed, the son of perdition." Many people have been led to a mid- or posttribulationist position because of this mistranslation (since it seems to teach that Christians will "fall away" during the tribulation). John Walvoord in his classic book *The Rapture Question* quotes another prophecy teacher about this verse:

> It is normally considered a reference to doctrinal apostasy. English pointed out that the word is derived from the verb *aphistemi*, used fifteen times in the New Testament, with only three of the references relating to religious departure. In eleven of the instances, the word *depart* is a good translation. As English indicated in a note, a number of ancient versions, such as Tyndale's, the Coverdale Bible, the version by Cranmer, the Geneva Bible, and Beza's translation, all from the sixteenth century, render the term "departing." He therefore suggested the possibility of rendering 2 Thessalonians 2:3 to the effect that the departure must "come first," i.e., the rapture of the church must occur before the man of sin is revealed. If this translation be admitted, it would constitute an explicit statement that the rapture of the church occurs before the Tribulation.*

---

* John F. Walvoord, *The Rapture Question* (Grand Rapids: Zondervan Publishing House, 1970), pp. 67-68.

Deliverance of Christians from the world's greatest period of wrath is a gift of God for His church. It is not something she deserves, but something He gives because He loves His church. In Ephesians Paul uses the symbol of a bride and groom to illustrate the relationship of Christ and His church, which is called "the bride of Christ." It is like the perfect Groom to manifest His love by rapturing His church before the period of wrath just because He loves her. Scripture and the love of Christ seem to favor the pretribulationist view of the rapture.

CHAPTER 10

Not Really So Obscure

✦

One of the criticisms of the pretribulation rapture view is that the rapture is not directly mentioned very many times in Scripture. (It appears in John 14:1-3; 1 Thessalonians 4:13-18; 1 Corinthians 15:50-56; 2 Thessalonians 2:1-12; and possibly Revelation 4:1,2.)

In addition, while we are told five times in Scripture that we are "kept from wrath," scores of other Scriptures refer to the final physical coming of Christ. But my question is, "How many times does the Bible have to teach something for it to be accepted as fact?" You may be surprised to learn that the term "born again" occurs only three times in Scripture! Yet few Bible scholars deny its necessity to get into the kingdom of God.

Actually, the Bible has to mention a matter *only once* for it to be a divine fact. We have more than enough biblical evidence to believe that the second coming is in two phases. The rapture phase will occur prior to the tribulation; when our Lord calls His church to come up to Himself. The second phase will occur seven years later, at the end of the tribulation; when Christ comes physically to reign on the earth.

Some critics ridicule pretribulationists by saying that no

one passage teaches it all; we must take bits and pieces of Scripture and weave them together to come to the pre-tribulation position. However, I question this allegation because I have found this teaching in one verse, in one chapter, and in one book. Let's examine these passages.

The Rapture in One Verse

In Titus 2:13, in the midst of a hard-hitting challenge to God's people to live a holy and godly life, Paul challenges them on the basis of the anticipation of the second coming of our Lord with these words: "looking for the *blessed hope* and the *glorious appearing* of our great God and Savior Jesus Christ...."

The blessed hope is very definitely a reference to the rapture of the church. Examined from every angle, the rapture immediately following the resurrection of dead believers is a "blessed hope." The hope of the church is not to triumph here on this earth, or even be in the majority. Our "hope" or confident expectation is that one day we are going to win in this race called life, not through anything we have done but because according to His mercy He saves us out of this world before the time of wrath begins.

As I pointed out in the previous chapter, if looking forward to His coming means going through the tribulation with all its woes, judgments, trumpets, bowls, and catastrophes, it is no "blessed hope" at all. Interestingly enough, the "blessed hope" or rapture is always mentioned in a context of joy.

Consider our Lord's challenge to His disciples the night before He died. He did not say, "Buck up, men; don't let your hearts be troubled just because you have to go through the tribulation before I can take you to be with myself." Instead He said, "Let not your heart be troubled.... I will come again and receive you to Myself, that where I am, there you may be also" (John 14:1,3). This is saying the same thing Paul meant when he said, "The Lord Himself shall descend.... Then we who are alive and remain shall be caught up... to meet the Lord in the air" (1 Thessalonians 4:16,17). The rapture is truly a *blessed hope* for the church.

The glorious appearing is quite a different matter. It is that special day when Christ will be acknowledged by all as "King of Kings and Lord of Lords." It is obviously the literal physical stage of His second coming. (We will dedicate a whole chapter to this topic.)

So Titus 2:13 shows both phases of the Lord's coming in one verse.

PRETRIBULATIONISM IN ONE CHAPTER

Second Thessalonians 2:1-12 contains the rapture, tribulation, and glorious appearing in one chapter. The whole subject is referred to in the first verse as "the coming of our Lord Jesus Christ." Then Paul uses a conjunction that is usually translated "and," but which can also be translated "even." In either case he refers to "our gathering together to Him." The "second coming" is a reference to the entire coming of Christ, including the two phases separated by seven years. Our gathering together to Him cannot mean the glorious appearing, since that is when all living creatures are gathered to Him for the judgment of the nations and the establishment of His kingdom. So in verse 1 we have both the glorious appearing and the "gathering together to Him" (the rapture). Turn now to the next study guide and locate for yourself the events in these 12 verses. (You may want to write lightly so you can work all the events in, and then, when you complete them, go back and darken them.)

STUDY GUIDE 15

Our Gathering Together to Christ
2 Thessalonians 2:1-12

✦

Locate the following: The day of Christ (verse 2).

What two things must come before that day (verse 3)?

_____

What two names do you find in this verse for Antichrist
(verse 3)? _____

_____

List the two things he will do (verse 4).
1) _____
2) _____

What is Antichrist called in verse 8? _____

When is he "revealed"? _____

What will finally happen to him? _____

When will it happen? _____

_____

Who will really be behind him (verse 9)? _____

How do you account for the supernatural signs he will perform during the tribulation period? _____

_____

What will he do to the unsaved (verse 10)? _____

_____

Why (verse 10)? _____

_____

What does God do to them (verse 11)? _____

_____

Give two things that cause this action by God (verse 12).

1) _____

2) _____

_____

✦

GOD WILL SEND DELUSION

In looking back over these 12 verses of 2 Thessalonians 2, you find that we have the rapture, the tribulation, and the glorious appearing—all in one chapter (study Figure 7 carefully).

This is an astonishing thought in Scripture! God is not in the business of sending delusion; He is a revealer of truth. That is why He gave us the Bible, His revelation to mankind. He has also given us the Holy Spirit to guide Christians into truth and to convict the unsaved. Yet here He

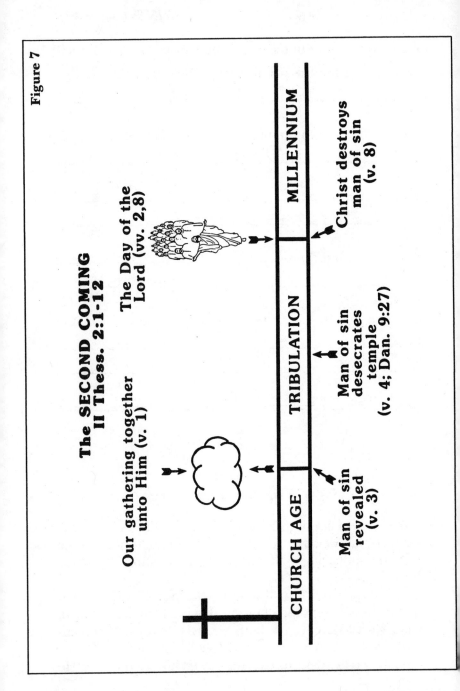

Figure 7

sends strong delusion "so that they believe the lie." The lie, of course, will be the Antichrist's gospel, which will be taught by the False Prophet and his followers (Revelation 13).

To understand who the Lord is talking about here, you have to go back to the principle of Hebrews 11:6, that "without faith it is impossible to please God." During this church age faith has to be sparked by the Word of God. In Luke 16 Christ quoted Abraham talking to the lost rich man about why Lazarus could not go back from the dead to warn his unbelieving brothers not to come to this place of torment: "They have Moses and the prophets; let them hear them." We have even more: We have the words of Jesus and His apostles. So during the church age it is not by signs and wonders that people are to be saved, but by the preaching of the Word of God.

The people of 2 Thessalonians 2:9-12 are unsaved people who go into the tribulation period in spite of the fact that they heard the gospel, the Word of God, but refused to believe "because they had pleasure in unrighteousness." Doubtless you know individuals who have rejected Christ because they love sin and refuse to give it up to follow Him. If they have heard the Word, they probably know about the rapture. When it occurs, millions of people will be missing on the same day. This obvious miracle will confirm the facts of Scripture that today are accepted by believers by faith. In addition, during the tribulation period (especially in the first 42 months) they will know of the supernatural signs and wonders of the two witnesses and the testimony of the 144,000 converted Jews. With their understanding of the gospel of the church age they will realize that these things are happening just as the Bible said they would. Salvation would not be an act of great faith for them; they would be responding mostly by sight. Consequently the signing of the covenant between Israel and the Antichrist will be the signal that they delayed their last chance to accept Christ by faith. At the point God will send them strong delusion so that they will permanently reject what they know to be true. It is a sad picture, and should motivate us to double our efforts to reach the lost with the gospel while there is still time.

PRETRIBULATIONISM IN ONE BOOK

The book of Revelation was written by John about 50 years after the Lord founded His church and ascended to heaven. In it John not only revealed Jesus Christ in His present and future state but also gave an outline of "things to come." The book flows from the days of John right up to the coming of Christ in power and beyond.

Chapter 1 is the introduction, while chapters 2 and 3 cover the church age. Seven historical churches are used to describe the entire church age. For example, the church of Ephesus is the only one that refers to apostles, because that first-century church was the only one that had apostles in it. We do not have space to consider all seven churches; for that, please see the author's book *Revelation Illustrated and Made Plain* (Zondervan Publishing House, 1975).

Chapters 4 and 5 are scenes in heaven. Then, as we have already studied, chapters 6 to 18 give the most detailed description of the events of the tribulation period to be found in the Bible. In chapter 19 Christ comes physically to the earth, judging the Antichrist, the False Prophet, and the nations. In chapter 20 He binds Satan in the bottomless pit. He then sets up His thousand-year kingdom on earth, followed by the judgment of the lost of all ages. The last two chapters (21 and 22) describe the eternal heaven that Christ has prepared for believers of all ages. The book is a chronological description of events from the beginning of the church to eternity (see Figure 8.)

Going back to the end of the church age, chapters 2 and 3 of Revelation describe events that will happen on the earth, while chapters 4 and 5 present a brief description of heaven just prior to the beginning of the tribulation. Notice what happens to John, a member of the church age, in 4:1,2:

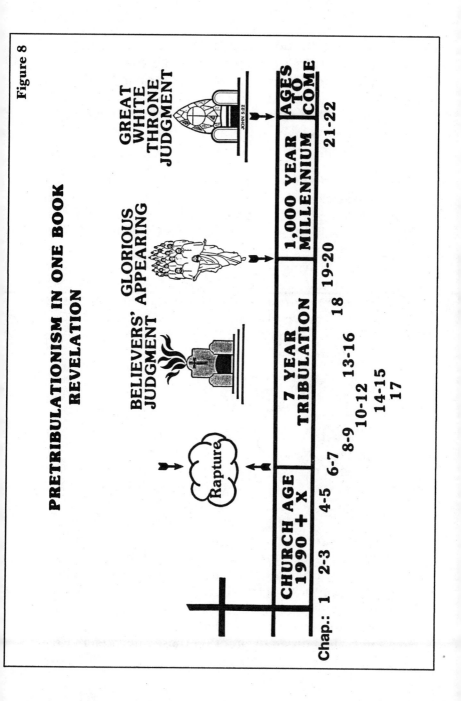

Figure 8

> After these things I looked, and behold, a door standing open in heaven. And the first voice which I heard was like a trumpet speaking with me, saying, "Come up here, and I will show you things which must take place after this." Immediately I was in the Spirit; and behold, a throne set in heaven, and One sat on the throne.

John is translated from the earthly scenes he has described to heaven *before* the tribulation begins. This passage alone would not establish the rapture as a pretribulational event, but in light of the passages we have studied that describe the rapture and the translation of all believers (both dead and living) at this stage of Christ's coming, John being called up into heaven could certainly be a clear implication of the pretribulation rapture. John is at least a symbol of the church when she is raptured to be with Christ "in the air" while the people still living on earth go through the tribulation period.

THE CHURCH IS NOT IN
THE TRIBULATION

An additional reason for believing that the church will not go through the tribulation period is that nowhere in the many prophetic passages of Scripture is the church shown in the tribulation. This is highly significant in view of the passages which we have already examined that promise that Christians are "saved from wrath." Nowhere is this more significant than in the book of Revelation, where the church is mentioned *13 times* in the first three chapters. Then, after John is called up into heaven and the world goes through the tribulation period, the church is not mentioned even *once* until chapter 19, when she is seen coming with Christ to "rule and reign with Him." This silence from chapters 6 to 18 puts the burden of proof on those interpreters who insist that the church does go through all or part of the tribulation. They should be able to identify the church in tribulation passages. So far I have not seen anyone do so.

SUMMARY

The church should not be expecting the tribulation period, although the Jewish people should. They have seven prophetic years still unfulfilled, and these years will be fulfilled during that time of wrath called "the time of Jacob's trouble." The unsaved Gentiles should also expect that time when "the new world order" for a one-world government will come on the scene saying, "Let's give world peace a chance." All it would take is for a charismatic-type world figure who has no place for God or His moral values to pull it all together through the United Nations or some other such international organization, and it could begin.

Christians are not looking for that time of wrath. We are looking for the coming of our Lord, and we should so live that if He raptures His church "at such a time as you think not," we will be ready. And certainly every unsaved person who has heard the gospel and understands it should call on the name of the Lord for salvation, "lest these days come upon him as a thief and he be left behind."

More important than any other question on prophecy is this: If Christ comes today to rapture His church and then commence His tribulation period, will you be ready to be caught up with Him in the air? If not, you can make yourself ready by personally inviting Christ into your heart by faith.

CHAPTER 11

Our Lord's Outline of Prophecy

✦

The Olivet Discourse, which was given by our Lord to His disciples on the Mount of Olives the day before His crucifixion, is probably the most important single prophecy passage in the New Testament. It is mentioned in Matthew 24 and 25, Mark 13, and Luke 21. If properly understood, this passage provides a basic outline upon which all other prophetic passages can be located. For that reason we should study it in detail.

This whole teaching came about in response to two questions which the disciples asked Jesus. They had evidently visited Jerusalem and showed Him the temple buildings which had been restored by Herod the Great just a few years before. Verse 1 of Matthew 24 indicates that the disciples "came to Him to show Him the buildings of the temple." He evidently was not as impressed with the building as they were, for He immediately predicted the destruction of that temple. His prophecy was fulfilled less than 40 years later, when the armies of Titus the Roman general surrounded the city, laid a long and torturous siege to it, and finally conquered it. Titus then totally destroyed the city—and the temple.

One interesting sidelight here is that Jesus not only predicted that the temple would be destroyed, but in verse 2 He added, "I say to you, not one stone shall be left here upon another that shall not be thrown down." Today that specific prophecy can be verified by a visit to Jerusalem and the famous "Wailing Wall," which is made of the stones of the temple. Every stone was taken down and removed from the entire temple site, and then some of those same stones were used over a thousand years later to erect what is now called the "Wailing Wall." (This wall is located just off the temple site.) Since the stones are so enormous, each one had to be moved one at a time, thereby fulfilling Christ's prophecy that "there would not be one stone left upon another." This fact has no immediate bearing on the prophecy passage that is about to follow except that it dramatizes the historic accuracy with which our Lord's words were fulfilled. If that one explicit prophecy was fulfilled, we can anticipate that the sweeping panorama of prophecy He was about to give will be equally fulfilled.

STUDY GUIDE 16

The Olivet Discourse

♦

Evidently Jesus and His disciples walked from the temple site across the Kidron Valley to the Mount of Olives, where the disciples asked Christ two very significant questions that sparked this prophecy. Being Jews who were probably familiar with Daniel 9 and Zechariah 14, they understood that before the coming of Messiah the city of Jerusalem would be surrounded by an enemy army, the city destroyed, and the temple desecrated. Then Messiah would come in great power to set up His kingdom. Their understanding of these prophecies is seen in the questions they asked. What were these questions?

Matthew 24:3b: _____

Matthew 24:3c: _____

Note Jesus' warning in verse 4: _____

What two deceptions were they to beware of?

1) (verse 5): _____

2) (verse 6a): _____

_____

What should be the reaction of Christians to "wars and rumors of wars" (verse 6b)? _____

Why (verse 6c)? _____

Temporarily skipping their first question, Jesus began answering their second What are the four parts of "the sign of Your coming"?

1) (verse 7a): _____

2) (verse 7b): _____

3) (verse 7c): _____

4) (verse 7d): _____

✦

Evidently, ordinary wars and rumors of wars, which have plagued man for 2000 years, were not "the sign." A special kind of war would occur that involved many nations, followed by the other three parts of the sign mentioned in verse 7, and this would be "the sign." Can you think of such a war? _____

Verse 8 is derived from a Hebrew idiom meaning "the beginning of travail" (like birth pains). One leads to another, and they increase in intensity until the child is born.

Now read Matthew 24 and locate each event and the verses covered by it as best you can on Figure 9. Include also the events covered in Matthew 25:31-46. Do not look at my end-of-chapter chart (Figure 10) for comparison until you have designed your own chart! Then compare them. If you have difficulty locating an event, move on to the next section and then return to it.

One thing you will discover here is that because the disciples were Jews and had no understanding of the rapture, and because the events described (except for the signs) will occur after the rapture, it is not mentioned in this passage. Our Lord's view here was primarily of what would happen to *Israel* at the end of the age. However, it would be helpful if you located the rapture in dotted lines (as we have already seen it taught from other passages) at the place you think it will occur on the chart.

THE SIGN SUMMARY

Our Lord answered the disciples' two questions "What will be THE sign of Your coming, and of the end of the age?" They merged these two ideas together, thinking of the glorious appearing of Messiah, whom the Orthodox Jews to this day expect to come in glorious power, destroying the enemies of Israel and then setting up the "kingdom of Israel" promised by many Old Testament prophets.

Our Lord warned His disciples to take heed that they not be deceived by false messiahs. He knew that many false messiahs would come, deceiving many (and they have), but they are not *the sign*. Then He injected the subject of war, but said that *the sign* was not just an ordinary war, like the hundreds that have occurred since He left this world. Instead, He predicted that there would be a special kind of

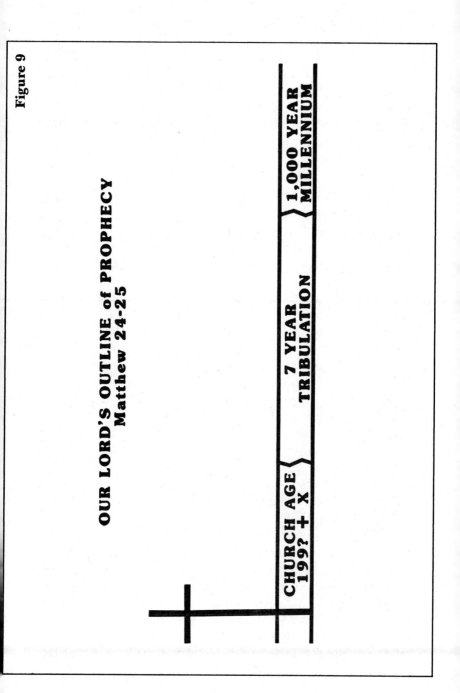

Figure 9

OUR LORD'S OUTLINE of PROPHECY
Matthew 24-25

CHURCH AGE
1992 + X

7 YEAR
TRIBULATION

1,000 YEAR
MILLENNIUM

war beginning with one nation rising against another until they were joined by the kingdoms of the world. But even that was not the entire sign. That was just the first quarter, which if followed by famines, pestilence, and earthquakes in various places at the same time would be the first sign (*the sign* of His coming).

Then Jesus used an interesting idiom: the first birth pain of a woman in travail. The first birth pain would lead to another, and they would become intense until "the end." Other signs regarding the end of the age and the Lord's coming are given in several other Scripture passages. For a detailed study of these many signs, please see the author's book *The Beginning of the End* (Tyndale House Publishers, 1981).

Before we get to the subsequent events, I should point out that historically there has been only one event that comes close to fulfilling all these qualifications—World War I, which was followed by unprecedented famines, pestilences, and earthquakes. But this alone does not mean that it was *the sign*, although many Christians thought for years that it was. Israel went back into her land (starting in 1916) as promised in Ezekiel 36, Russia became a dominant world power (starting in 1917) as prophesied in Ezekiel 38 and 39, and other seeming fulfillments began to occur. However, since Matthew 24:34 indicates that the generation that sees the fulfillment of *the sign* "will by no means pass away till all these things are fulfilled," this interpretation is not as popular as it once was, since very few of those old-timers who saw the First World War still remain. As long as some of those old-timers, born around 1900, still remain, that interpretation remains a possibility, but at present it doesn't seem as probable as it once did.

On the other hand, it could be that these events were just a sample of a world war that will yet fulfill all the requirements of *the sign*, thereby indicating that "it is near, even at the very doors." That could conceivably be World War III, which, God forbid, could come in our lifetime.

Another popular view held by many students of prophecy is that the "fig tree" mentioned in Matthew 24:32 is the sign. They suggest that since the fig tree, when used symbolically, refers to Israel, then the regathering of Israel is the sign. Verse 7 could then be "the beginning of sorrows" or the first birth pain of the sign, although verse 32 is really *the sign*, per se. They point out that although some Jews were in the land prior to World War I, it took the signing of the Balfour Treaty in 1916 to cause thousands of Jews to begin gathering back into the land of Israel, and that the sign of fulfillment occurred in 1948, when Israel was recognized as a sovereign country by the United Nations. If so, then there is plenty of time remaining during which the "generation" of verse 34 that saw Israel established as a nation back in the land could survive, or "by no means pass away till all these things are fulfilled." That could be another 40 to 50 years, or even more.

You may wonder at all this ambiguity regarding the sign and which generation would be alive when the Lord comes. (Remember that they too, just like ourselves, were interested in "the sign of Your coming.") But our Lord warned them, "Of that day and hour no one knows, no, not even the angels of heaven, but My Father only" (verse 36). It is not God's will that we know "the day or the hour"! That is why date-setters can always be branded as wrong, and why those who have set dates have brought unnecessary embarrassment on the church. However, it is possible that some generation that sees all the parts of these signs fall into place can "know that summer is near." That is, they can know that the "season" is approaching.

Ours may not be the generation that participates in the rapture—yet again it could be. Why? Because our generation has more prophetic reason, through fulfilled prophecy, to believe that Christ is coming than any generation since Christ ascended and promised to return.

Now we turn back to what happens next after *the sign*. Verse 9 introduces the tribulation and subsequent events.

You will find that this flows in parallel with our previous studies of that seven-year period. Now, please fill in Study Guide 17.

STUDY GUIDE 17

Matthew Chapters 24 and 25

✦

Have verses 9-14 ever been fulfilled in history? _____

List five things that will happen during the first half of the tribulation.

1) _____

2) _____

3) _____

4) _____

5) _____

What good news is found in verse 14? _____

_____

Verse 15 is a very important event. Read Daniel 9:27, 11:31, and 12:11, which are parallel verses, and then describe the events.

_____

_____

_____

Locate these events on your chart. What does Jesus tell the Jews living at that time to do (verses 16-20)? _____

_____

What does our Lord call this new phase of the tribulation period (verse 21)? _____

_____

List some of the characteristics of that age as described in verses 21-26. _____

_____

What does verse 27 tell us about Christ's second coming?

_____

List five miracles that will happen when Christ returns (verses 29,30a).

1) _____
2) _____
3) _____
4) _____
5) _____

Why do the "tribes mourn" (verse 30)? _____

_____

Describe "the elect" of verse 31. _____

_____

_____

In verse 32, what parable to you learn from the fig tree in light of verse 36? _____

_____

What is Christ teaching in verses 37-39 and 40-44? _____

_____

_____

What is His conclusion (verses 45-47)? _____

_____

What happens to those who reject Him (verses 48-51)?

_____

Briefly summarize the judgment of the nations described in 25:31-46.

_____

_____

_____

✦

TRIBULATION SUMMARY
MATTHEW 24:9-31

We have already seen that our Lord's Olivet Discourse in Matthew 24 and 25 is the most important passage of prophecy in the New Testament. If you understand this passage you will be able to locate most of the events in other prophecies. Matthew 24:9-31 provides essential details of the tribulation period right up to the second coming of Christ to the earth to set up His literal, physical kingdom. This is amazingly compatible with Revelation chapters 6 to 19 and 2 Thessalonians 2:1-12, which we have already studied.

You will recall that the disciples asked the Lord, "What will be *the sign* of Your coming and the end of the age?" They merged the two events together because at that point they had never been told about the rapture of the church. So the Lord gave them the sign, which as we have seen will be a monstrous world war followed by famines, pestilences, and earthquakes, similar to the historic World War I period. Then He called that event the "beginning of travail" or "first birth pain," a Hebrew idiom of a woman in travail. This symbolizes a process of time interspersed by several other "birth pains" or events of history that fulfill prophecy. Matthew 24:9 then introduces what follows that sign without giving the length of it. Then in verse 32, where Christ takes up the subject of the sign again, He tells the parable of the fig tree (which may mean the establishment of Israel) and warns the disciples that "summer is near," "at the very doors."

Admittedly, this is complex and difficult to understand. But the best suggestion I have seen is that taking the expression "This generation [that sees this sign] will by no means pass away till all these things are fulfilled" (verse 34) could mean that the generation which saw that special war referred to in verse 7 would not pass until the tribulation and the glorious appearing "are fulfilled."

The generation that saw the First World War of 1914-1918 (which was interestingly enough followed by famines, pestilences, and earthquakes) has almost vanished from the earth. Just a few million people who were approximately ten years old in 1914 (so they could see those events) are still alive. They would be around 85 years old today. However, Christ said they would see "*all* these things fulfilled," which would include the seven-year tribulation period. So we must add another seven years to their age, making them about 92 or older. While there are many people still living in their mid-nineties (some of whom may live to be over 100), every day that passes finds fewer of that generation. Consequently, although that interpretation is still possible, it becomes increasingly unlikely.

If, on the other hand, verse 7 is just describing the fact that the 2000 years of present history would be filled with war after war, along with famines, pestilences, and earthquakes, but that "the fig tree" parable, which began by an agreement during the first World War (the Balfour Treaty) and culminated with the 1948 establishment of the nation of Israel, is really *the sign*, then another 30 to 50 (or more) years can be added to "the generation that sees all these things."

Whichever interpretation is taken is not nearly so important as the fact that the coming of Christ for His church could very well "be near, even at the doors." This fact should characterize the way we live! More important than *when* He comes is the fact that He *is* coming and that Christians should be *ready* for Him when He arrives.

After He comes, according to verse 9, the tribulation period begins here on earth (or at least that portion of the tribulation covered in Revelation 6 and 7, when the world leader makes a covenant with Israel for seven years which he breaks after 3½ years). During that tribulation time believers will experience difficult days of opposition, false Christs, and lawlessness. But the gospel of the kingdom will be preached around the world, probably by the 144,000 Jewish witnesses of Revelation 7, who reach "a great multitude which no one could number, of all nations, tribes, peoples, and tongues."

Matthew 24:15 portrays the "abomination of desolation," when the Antichrist desecrates the rebuilt temple in Jerusalem. (Obviously it has to be rebuilt in order to be desecrated.) That desecration comes in the middle of the tribulation period and triggers what our Lord called "The Great Tribulation," which will be the worst time in the history of the world for anyone who believes in God and refuses to bow down and worship "the beast" or the one-world government leader called Antichrist.

That period culminates at the end of the 7-year period with the coming of Christ in power to establish His kingdom on earth—which we shall yet study. The important message of our Lord to everyone here, and especially the church, is to live a holy life and be ready for whenever our Lord comes, so we will not have any regrets when we face Him. Jesus said, "Watch therefore, for you do not know what hour your Lord is coming." He also said, "Occupy *till I come!*"

Study the chart in Figure 10 carefully and compare it with your own.

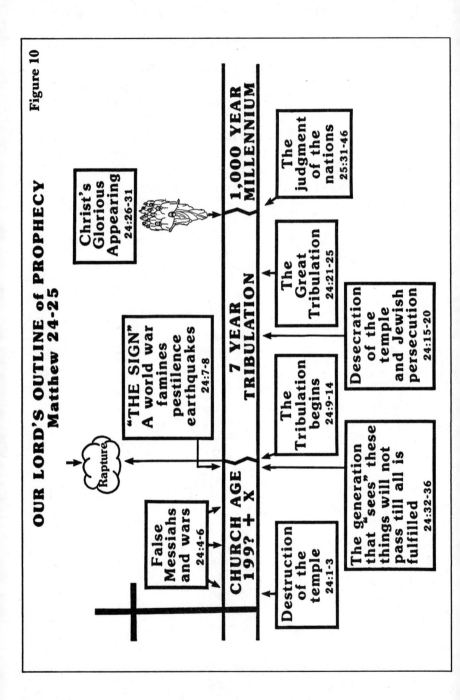

OUR LORD'S OUTLINE of PROPHECY
Matthew 24-25

Figure 10

Christ's Glorious Appearing
24:26-31

1,000 YEAR MILLENNIUM

The judgment of the nations
25:31-46

The Great Tribulation
24:21-25

7 YEAR TRIBULATION

"THE SIGN"
A world war famines pestilence earthquakes
24:7-8

Desecration of the temple and Jewish persecution
24:15-20

The Tribulation begins
24:9-14

Rapture

False Messiahs and wars
24:4-6

CHURCH AGE 199? + X

The generation that "sees" these things will not pass till all is fulfilled
24:32-36

Destruction of the temple
24:1-3

CHAPTER 12

The Christian Resurrection from the Dead

✦

Belief in life after death is not unique to Christianity. It is so ingrafted into human intuition that every religion in the world is built on that expectation—as though the Creator wanted man to know that once born, human beings are eternal. From the primitive tribesmen of the jungles to the sophisticated Oriental mystics, every tradition has some system of belief in the afterlife.

For some people, like the American Indians, it is just another life in "the happy hunting grounds." For others, like the Hindu religion, it is a complex tale of several afterlives in a higher or lower caste system here on earth, depending on how a person lived. The good come back in a higher caste; the bad come back lower. The Parsis of India wear masks over their mouths so they won't swallow a gnat and by chance inhale their grandfather who happened to be such a degenerate that he came back in the bug caste.

Christianity tells without doubt the most beautiful story of life in the afterlife—for believers. Our Bible gives far more interesting and believable details about the next life than any other source, including Judaism, which is similar but lacks many of the details revealed only in the New Testament by our Lord and His disciples. That should not be surprising since only Christianity has a Bible that came from God Himself, some parts of which were revealed personally by His own Son, who said, "I have come that they may have life, and that they may have it more abundantly" (John 10:10).

To show you how deeply entrenched in the Old Testament Scriptures the subject of bodily resurrection was, answer the questions in the next study guide.

STUDY GUIDE 18

The Old Testament Teaching on Resurrection

✦

Job was the first person to ever record a biblical reference to the resurrection. He is considered to be the most knowledgeable man in the first 2000 years of recorded history regarding the ways of God. Study Job 19:25-27 and answer the following questions.

What two things did Job know about God (verse 25)? ___

_____

_____

In what condition did Job expect to see God after his death (verse 26)? _____

_____

What would be his relationship to God at the time (verse 27)? _____

_____

Abraham, the father of the Hebrew race and quite possibly the most venerated of all the Old Testament patriarchs (since more space is given to him in the New Testament than to any Old Testament leader), must have believed in resurrection.

In the book of Hebrews, the Holy Spirit revealed that Abraham looked for something after death. What was it (11:10)?

_____

_____

In what state did he believe life would be in the next world (11:19)? _____

_____

King David, the psalm-writer, lived about a thousand years before Christ and described his beliefs in the next life. Study Psalm 16:7-11.

How did David face death (verse 9)? _____

_____

_____

What did he mean by verse 10? _____

_____

What did he expect in the future (verse 11)? _____

_____

Would that be possible without resurrection? _____

_____

Daniel, one of the greatest and most righteous men in the Bible, said what of death in Daniel 12:2? _____

_____

How does he describe "awake"? _____

Jewish tradition at the time of Christ: In John 11:24, Martha, the sister of Lazarus (whom Jesus raised from the dead), reflected the view of her generation. What was it?

_____

_____

To this day the Jews hold the same view that Martha expressed to Jesus. Is that statement compatible with the Christian view? _____

_____

_____

✦

SUMMARY

Christianity is a religion of resurrection. Our Lord gave His own resurrection as the paramount sign of His deity (Matthew 12:39). His disciples, a defeated lot after His crucifixion, were motivated to world evangelism by His resurrection. In fact, all of them except John were martyred for their testimony that they had personally seen Christ alive after His resurrection. Not only the apostles saw Him, but as Luke said, "He presented Himself alive after His suffering by many infallible proofs" (Acts 1:3) over a period of 40 days after His resurrection. On one occasion He was seen by 120 people in the upper room, and at another time (possibly His ascension) He was seen by about 500 people at once (1 Corinthians 15:6). It was the fact of the resurrection that motivated these disciples and apostles to "turn the world upside down" by their Spirit-empowered evangelism and the testimony that the angels gave: "He is not here, for He is risen, as He said!" (Matthew 28:6).

In addition, Christ taught on several occasions that the graves of believers would open and come forth to "everlasting life." (See John 5:21,24 as just one example.) In John 11, just prior to raising Lazarus from the dead (the third such person He raised). Christ distinctly tied Himself to the fact of resurrection with these words: "I am the resurrection and the life. He who believes in Me, though he may die, he shall live. And whoever lives and believes in Me shall never die" (John 11:25,26).

Without question, it is impossible to remove Jesus Christ from resurrection. It is a doctrinal necessity in that if there is no resurrection, Christianity is a fraud; Christ would not be divine, and, as Paul said, "You are still in your sins" (1 Corinthians 15:17). But since He *did* rise from the dead, we have His promise, "Because I live, you will live also!" (John 14:19).

STUDY GUIDE 19

The Christian View of Resurrection
1 Corinthians 15

✦

How important to Christianity is the resurrection of the body?

Verse 13: _____

_____

Verse 14a: _____

_____

Verse 14b: _____

_____

Verse 15a: _____

_____

Verse 15b: _____

_____

Verse 16: _____

_____

Verse 17: _____

_____

Verse 18: _____

_____

If there is no resurrection, what are we (verse 19)? _____

_____

There are distinct orders of resurrection. What are they?

_____

Verse 20,23a: _____

_____

Verse 23b: _____

_____

Verse 24: _____

_____

_____

STUDY GUIDE 20

The Resurrected Body
1 Corinthians 15

✦

_____

Why is our present body unable to go right to heaven or the millennial kingdom (15:35-42)? _____

_____

Verse 43: _____

_____

What kind of body will it be (verse 44)? _____

_____

Does this mean it will not be a real body that is recognizable or can talk? See Colossians 3:4. _____

_____

First Corinthians 15:47-49 gives more details. What are they? _____

_____

Why must our body be changed (verse 50)? _____

_____

What is Paul's "mystery" (verses 51-53)? _____

_____

_____

STUDY GUIDE 21

Resurrection Before Rapture

✦

When Christ comes to rapture His church, there will be two kinds of Christians. Who are they? Compare 1 Corinthians 15:52 and 1 Thessalonians 4:13a. _____

_____

_____

Who are the people referred to in 4:14b? _____

_____

Who does Paul mean in 4:15a? _____

_____

Who in 4:15b? _____

_____

Summarize the two classes of Christians you find in this passage.

1) _____

2) _____

What will *not* happen (verse 15)? _____

_____

What is the one condition required to be a part of this resurrection (4:14)? _____

_____

What is that called in 1 Corinthians 15:1-3? _____

_____

_____

✦

OLD TESTAMENT SAINTS
AND TRIBULATION SAINTS

The Bible is not entirely clear on whether Old Testament saints will be included in the rapture. Some believe it is only for the church, and that Old Testament believers who looked forward to the cross by faith will remain in the grave until the glorious appearing. That may account for the fact that they are not specifically mentioned in any rapture passage. The rapture may just be for the church, which would fit the overall plan of God's dealing with Israel in the Old Testament, as separate from His dealing specifically with the church for almost 2000 years. (During the last seven years He will go back to specifically leading Israel in a personal way during "the time of Jacob's trouble." Then, at the end of the tribulation, He will resurrect the dead Old Testament saints and the tribulation saints, who are joined together with the church to go with Christ into the millennium.)

The resurrection-rapture of the Old Testament saints may be what the psalmist foresaw in Psalm 50. There the Messiah is seen in the air calling back to heaven for the Old Testament saints and the believers who died during the tribulation. Then He gathers those on earth to Him by "changing their mortal bodies" as He comes to earth in His glorious appearing (Psalm 50:4,5). This would account for the resurrection of all believers of all time to that point. (The *millennial* saints will be resurrected and changed 1000 years later.)

SUMMARY

The Bible teaches that our present body is "corruptible"—that is, it is human or "natural." That is why we can still sin after we have been born again. At salvation, God's Spirit comes into our heart so that at the time of death our soul (the eternal part of our being) and our "new nature" or "spirit" departs to be with Christ, where it remains until the resurrection-rapture. Then when Christ descends from heaven "with a shout...and the dead in Christ will rise first. Then we who are alive and remain shall be caught up together with them in the clouds" (1 Thessalonians 4:16,17).

Then we shall all "meet the Lord in the air" and be with Him forever.

Those believers who happen to be alive when He comes in the air will also be "changed" in the rapture. Our bodies, like fellow believers before us who "are asleep in Jesus," are unfit for heaven, but must be changed "like His glorious body" was after His resurrection. That heavenly body will be made from the elements of our present bodies, or our former bodies in the case of dead believers. (Wherever these bodies are—in the ocean, the grave, etc.—they will be resurrected.) Elements are never lost; God can gather each body's elements from anyplace in the universe where they are on resurrection day and combine them with the soul and spirit forever.

This new resurrected body, made from the elements of our former body, will be recognizable, will be able to communicate with other saints, and will even be able to eat, for our Lord ate fish with His disciples after His resurrection. Yet His resurrected body was not subject to time or space; He could walk through walls and travel great distances as by the speed of thought. In this state we will forever be with the Lord. It is in this "immortal body" that we will "rule and reign" with Christ throughout the millennium, and after that go into heaven for the eternity to come.

You can ransack the libraries of the world and never find a more complete and inspiring description in any religion comparable to that "blessed hope" which God has prepared for those who love Him and have put their faith in His Son. This is what the Bible calls "the first resurrection."

I must ask you two important questions:

1) Will you be a part of that resurrection? You need to answer that question for yourself.

2) If you are a Christian, are you living the kind of life that Christ expects of you in preparation for either death or His coming? _____

_____

What you will do immediately after that resurrection or rapture will be the subject of our next chapter.

Note: Locate, with a dotted line, the resurrection of the believing dead when Christ comes in the rapture on Figure 11.

Figure 11

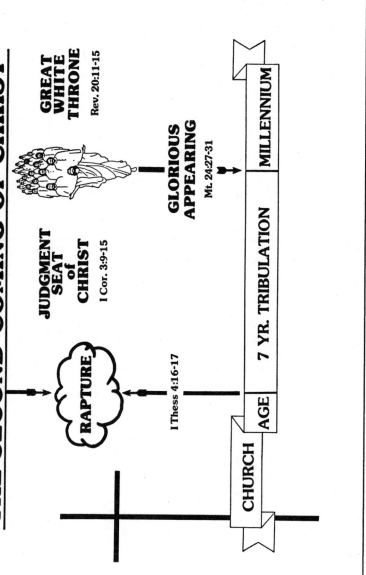

THE SECOND COMING OF CHRIST

GREAT WHITE THRONE
Rev. 20:11-15

JUDGMENT SEAT of CHRIST
I Cor. 3:9-15

GLORIOUS APPEARING
Mt 24:27-31

RAPTURE
I Thess 4:16-17

CHURCH AGE

7 YR. TRIBULATION

MILLENNIUM

CHAPTER 13

When Resurrected Christians Meet Their Lord

✦

Most Christians look forward to that incredible day when they will see their Lord. As we have already studied, God's plan for us, according to 1 Thessalonians 4:16,17, is to meet our dead loved ones and friends "in the clouds" first, then to meet the Lord "in the air."

Preachers have waxed eloquent describing both of those meetings. Like many Christians, I have two parents I long to meet in the clouds, along with many friends. But even that ecstatic moment will be eclipsed in the ecstasy of actually meeting the Lord who died for us, forgave us, saved us, led us through life, and resurrected us. Words cannot suffice to adequately describe that scene!

However, immediately after that event we will be judged by Him! Few Christians ever think about that. First Corinthians 4:5 says, "Judge nothing before the appointed time; wait till the Lord comes. He will bring to light what is hidden in darkness and will expose the motives of men's hearts" (NIV). Obviously, when the Lord comes He is going to judge His servants by examining their works and motives.

This meeting with our Lord in judgment is not an obscure teaching in Scripture. Keep in mind, however, that this judgment is not to determine whether we are saved or not, nor is it a judgment for sins committed prior to our salvation, for those sins were judged by God at Calvary when Christ died for those sins, and were forgiven the moment we confessed them (1 John 1:9). Instead, this judgment is to determine the rewards which believers will receive for faithful service after their salvation. But it's time for you to study it for yourself. Please fill in the next study guide.

STUDY GUIDE 22

Christians at the Judgment of Reward

✦

What is this judgment called (Romans 14:10-12)? _____

_____

Who will stand before the judge (14:12)? _____

_____

What do you think "account" means? _____

_____

What is it called in 2 Corinthians 5:10? _____

_____

Who will stand at that judgment? _____

_____

What is it for (5:12c)? _____

_____

So what should be our conclusion (5:9)? _____

_____

The most detailed description of this judgment seat for believers is found in 1 Corinthians 3:9-15. Locate it on the chart in Figure 12.

═══

STUDY GUIDE 23

The Judgment of Reward
1 Corinthians 3:9-15

✦

═══

What does Paul call Christians in verse 9? _____

_____

Who laid the foundation (verses 10,11)? _____

_____

What do you think that means? _____

_____

_____

Figure 12

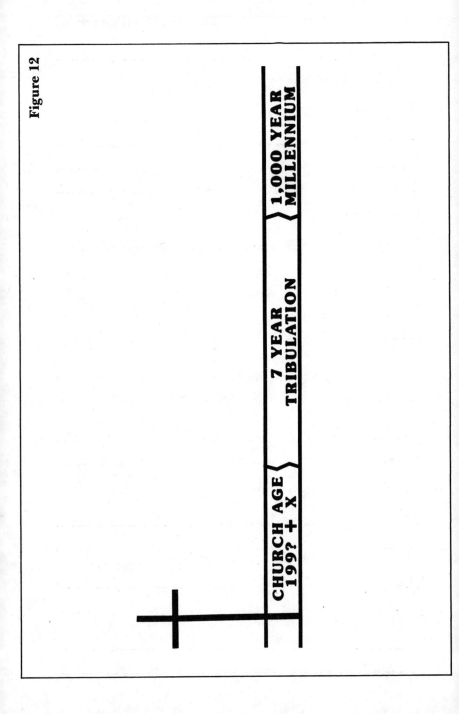

CHURCH AGE
199? + X

7 YEAR
TRIBULATION

1,000 YEAR
MILLENNIUM

List the six kinds of symbols Paul uses for good works in verse 12.

1) _____

2) _____

3) _____

4) _____

5) _____

6) _____

What will test those works (verse 13b)? _____

When (verse 13b)? _____

_____

What will it test for (verse 13c)? _____

_____

What happens if a believer's works survive the test (verse 14)? _____

_____

What happens if they don't (verse 15)? _____

_____

How would he be saved (verse 15b)? _____

_____

What does that mean? _____

_____

Write your own summary of this passage before reading mine.

_____

_____

_____

_____

_____

_____

_____

_____

✦

THE MISCONCEPTION ABOUT GOOD WORKS

Because we are saved "by grace...through faith, and that not of yourselves; it is the gift of God, not of works, lest anyone should boast" (Ephesians 2:8,9), many Christians think there is little or no call on their life today to serve our Lord. Consequently they accept His salvation as a gift and do nothing to advance His kingdom afterward. Unfortunately, they do not read on to the following verse: "For we are His workmanship, created in Christ Jesus for good works, which God prepared beforehand that we should walk in them" (Ephesians 2:10).

It is obvious by just reading this passage that the Lord expects His children to work for Him after they have been given salvation. In fact, we will be rewarded in the next life in direct proportion to the way we have served Him in this one.

STUDY GUIDE 24

What Are Good Works?

✦

What type of "good work" is mentioned in Matthew 5:16?

_____

What kind is mentioned in Matthew 26:7-10? _____

_____

What does "rich in good works" mean (1 Timothy 6:18)?

_____

Can only the rich give good works (Matthew 10:42)? ____

What does Christ consider a good work (Matthew 10:40-42)?

_____

What happens to those who do such works (verse 42c)?

_____

Such challenges are not uncommon in our Lord's teachings. He used many parables when addressing His disciples. Bible scholars define a parable as "an earthly story with a heavenly meaning." Since few people could imagine the kingdom of heaven, which believers will occupy during the millennium or "kingdom age," Jesus used stories they could understand so that they and we could draw an understandable parallel. Read the parables below and give a brief summary.

Parable of the talents: Matthew 25:14-30. _____

_____

_____

_____

Parable of the pounds: Luke 19:11-27. _____

_____

_____

_____

Parable of the wages: Matthew 20:1-16. _____

_____

_____

_____

What similarities do you find between these parables? __

_____

What differences are there in the rewards? _____

_____

What do you learn from Matthew 20:1-16 about the relationship between rewards and the length of time a believer has in this life to serve the Lord? _____

_____

_____

✦

SUMMARY OF JUDGMENT OF REWARD

Although Christians are given the free gift of salvation by a generous God, we are expected, once saved, to serve our Lord by doing good works. A good work can be anything done in the name of the Lord, or for His glory. It could be witnessing, worshiping Him, or even giving a "cup of cold water" in His name.

The symbolism in these parables is interesting in that Jesus compares Himself to a "householder" (landowner) or even a king who went on a long journey and after a "great while" (almost 2000 years?) returned—at which time he demanded of his servants an accounting and gave rewards according to their faithfulness, talent, and time spent in labor.

TALENT + GOSPEL + TIME = REWARD

My formula for this reward is: *Talent* times our productive sharing of the *gospel* times the *time* we had after our salvation to labor will equal our reward. The record of our works is kept by God, who knows what ability we have to serve Him, and will hold us accountable for how we use our talents and time for service. Fortunately, He is a just God and will treat each believer "according to his works," based on his or her natural ability.

Our Lord challenged us:

> Do not lay up for yourselves treasures on earth, where moth and rust destroy and where thieves break in and steal; but lay up for yourselves treasures in heaven, where neither moth nor rust destroys and where thieves do not break in and steal. For where your treasure is, there your heart will be also (Matthew 6:19-21).

In the mercy of God, He has not only given us salvation totally free, but He also gives us an opportunity to invest a portion of our "treasure" (our life) in eternal rewards. It seems that when we are saved, our Lord opens for us a bank account in heaven. All through our life we can deposit in that account "treasure" or "good works" done in His name and for His glory. Then when He comes we will stand before Him as He opens that account to see how much we have invested. He then will test it "by fire" to see how genuine it is.

According to 1 Corinthians 3:12,13, some of these works will be "gold, silver, or precious jewels," meaning that they will survive the fire test and the believer will receive a reward. (The rewards will be covered in a later summary.) But what you should also see in this passage is that "the wood, hay, and stubble" do not survive the fire test and the believer suffers loss of reward—not loss of salvation, but loss of *reward*. He will be saved "so as by fire," or as we might say "by the skin of his teeth." He will be saved, but his works will be lost.

BAD WORKS THAT ARE BURNED UP

The reason bad works don't qualify to abide the fire test and earn a reward is because they have not been done with the right spirit or motive. To the eye of man they may look like silver, gold, and precious stones, but in reality they are nothing but wood, hay, and stubble. The reality of the fire test will reveal "what sort it is," whether good or bad. The Scripture passages in Figure 13 provide some indication of what that means.

STUDY GUIDE 25

Don't Lose Your Rewards

✦

The average Christian believes that earned rewards, the

Figure 13

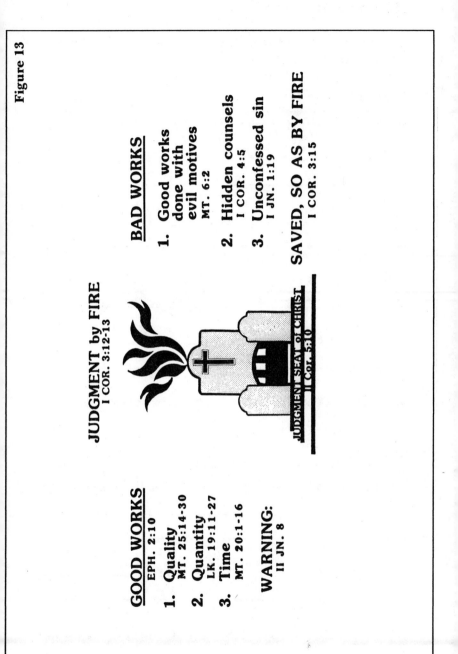

result of good works since his salvation, can never be lost. Evaluate these verses with that theory in mind.

1 Corinthians 3:14: _____

_____

What if his works don't endure the fire test? _____

_____

2 John 8: _____

_____

What is implied by "full reward"? _____

_____

Revelation 3:11 suggests what? _____

_____

What do you conclude from these three verses? _____

_____

If earned rewards can be lost or subtracted from, what could cause their loss? One insight will be the condition on which 1 John 1:9 is based. _____

_____

What if a person does not confess his sin? _____

_____

What could cause loss, based on 1 Corinthians 4:5? _____

_____

WHEN GOOD WORKS TURN TO STUBBLE

Read Matthew 6:2 and describe why some good works will receive no reward. _____

_____

_____

Ephesians 6:7 tells to whom service should be rendered:

_____

Colossians 3:17 tells who should be glorified by what we do: _____

_____

Colossians 3:23 makes it clear how good works should be done: _____

_____

Do you think some church work is done with this evil motive? _____

Give some examples. _____

_____

_____

According to these Scriptures and 1 Corinthians 3:14,15, will some believers who think they will receive rewards be surprised? _____

_____

✦

SUMMARY

Because our Lord challenged us to "lay up for yourselves treasure in heaven, where neither moth nor rust destroys and where thieves do not break in and steal," many Christians think that earned rewards are forever secure. What they do not realize is that although no other person or power can take these rewards from us, we can destroy them ourselves by the way we live.

I'm sure you are aware of certain well-known Christians who have served their Lord faithfully for many years but then through a moral indiscretion or some other sin brought reproach to the cause of Christ. The judgment seat of Christ will reveal all truth, even unconfessed failure and sin. If you recall, the works mentioned in 1 Corinthians 3 evidently all looked alike until after the fire "tested every man's work what sort it was." There would be no purpose in fire testing straw or wood or stubble—unless they looked the same as gold, silver, or jewels. It is the holy test of fire that determines whether the works were really "good or bad." To the church, a person's "Christian service" may look like good works, but his or her "evil motive" or "hidden counsels" will be revealed by Christ at this judgment, and the believer will lose his reward because his motive was one of self-seeking or hypocrisy.

The three verses we looked at in the previous study guide showed that a Christian can lose his crown, receive less than a full reward, and "suffer loss" even when expecting rewards. There are at least three things that could cause a loss of reward: unconfessed sin, good things done with an evil motive, and hidden counsels of the heart that are displeasing to God.

How all this will turn out is known only to God. But it does highlight the fact that God's work should be done in God's way—with a pure heart and a desire to glorify Him— or else there will be no reward, or at best a diminished reward. God is not interested in having us serve Him faithfully for just a few years, but rather for our entire lifetime. As Paul challenged Christians at the end of the great resurrection chapter which we have already studied, "Therefore, my beloved brethren, be steadfast, immovable, always abounding in the work of the Lord, knowing that your labor is not in vain in the Lord" (1 Corinthians 15:58).

For those whose faithful service provides them with genuine rewards that survive the fire test, Scripture promises crowns. Since the Bible tells us that we will reign with Christ (2 Timothy 2:12) when He comes in His kingdom, it is obvious what these crowns signify, for crowns are for rulers. That is compatible with His parable of the pounds, in which He promised to give rewards according to service by saying, "I will make you ruler over ten cities."

That may be the reason the judgment seat of Christ occurs just prior to the millennial kingdom—so that Christians can be assigned to opportunities of service according to the faithful use of their talents in directly or indirectly advancing Christ's spiritual kingdom in this life. But special insight can be gained by examining the different meanings for the crowns.

STUDY GUIDE 26

The Five Crowns for Service

✦

Read the text assigned and tell what kind of crown you think is referred to and how it is earned, and then compare your answer with the summary.

2 Timothy 4:8. _____

_____

_____

_____

1 Corinthians 9:25-27. _____

_____

_____

_____

What is the difference between these two crowns? _____

_____

_____

_____

James 1:12; Revelation 2:10. _____

_____

_____

_____

1 Thessalonians 2:19. _____

_____

_____

_____

1 Peter 5:4. _____

_____

_____

_____

Who wears crowns in this life? _____

_____

Who will wear them in the next life? _____

_____

_____

✦

CROWN SUMMARY

We have already seen that a crown is a symbol of ruler-ship and that these crowns are given on the basis of faithful service. As Paul challenged Timothy, "Make full proof of your ministry." In other words, take advantage of all your opportunities to use your talents to the maximum to advance God's kingdom while you have life on this earth. If faithful to His Lord, any Christian could earn at least one of these crowns. Many will earn several, although few (if any) will receive all.

THE CROWN OF RIGHTEOUSNESS
2 Timothy 4:8

The reason many Christians are not used by God is because they do not live a righteous life. It is not easy to live a righteous life in an unrighteous age; it is a constant fight. But the eternal reward will be well worth it. This verse suggests that if we live in the attitude that our Lord could come soon, we will be driven to live the kind of life He will approve.

THE INCORRUPTIBLE CROWN
1 Corinthians 9:25-27

This is often called "the victor's crown." It is different from the crown of righteousness that God expects of all Christians. This is the crown that is given to the faithful servant who denies himself and his personal desires in order to win the race in faithful service. He doesn't just avoid sin; in order to better serve his Lord, he avoids even some good things that other Christians enjoy.

Paul used runners as an illustration. They deny themselves personal time and relaxation to arduously train their body in order to win their race. Some Christians deny themselves financially to serve the Lord. I have often thought of teachers at Christian schools who scrimp on a tight budget because their salary is 25 to 50 percent lower than they would receive by teaching in the public sector. Missionaries have to deny themselves years of family contacts to bring the gospel to Bibleless tribes, and the list goes on.

This crown seems to be a reward for self-denial—a crown that few Christians in this self-indulgent age will receive.

Moses is a good example of a believer who will probably be given such a crown. While he could have remained as the number two man in Egypt, Scripture tells us:

> By faith Moses, when he became of age, refused to be called the son of Pharaoh's daughter, choosing rather to suffer affliction with the people of God than to enjoy the passing pleasures of sin, esteeming the reproach of Christ greater riches than the treasures in Egypt; for he looked to the reward (Hebrews 11:24-26).

THE CROWN OF LIFE

James 1:12 and Revelation 2:10 indicate that there is a special crown for those Christians who are persecuted for righteousness' sake. It is sometimes called "the martyr's crown," for it goes to those who have been cruelly killed because of their testimony and service for the Master.

God in His sovereignty has chosen to allow the martyrdom or persecution of some Christians during this church age, when He expects people to call on Him by faith in the teaching of His Word rather than by miracles and signs (such as were practiced during the first century, before the Bible was completed). While it seems unfair to us when such tragedies take place, be sure of this: All martyrs will be adequately compensated in the life to come. Like Moses, they will receive an eternal reward.

THE CROWN OF REJOICING

First Thessalonians 2:19 indicates that there is a special soul-winner's crown for those individuals who have majored in leading people to faith in Christ. Paul was like that. The people to whom he spoke were his "crown of rejoicing" because he had led them to Christ and taught them in the faith. Note the title: "rejoicing." That is the same term used of the angels in heaven who rejoice when one sinner comes to faith. In the light of eternity, soul-winning is the most important thing in the world. All this busy activity and the "things" of this earth pale into insignificance in the light of eternity, for in that day these things will be burned up and forgotten, and "only what's done for Christ will last."

Almost every church has those faithful individuals whose greatest joy is leading people to Christ. They are a minority, but they faithfully come out on "calling night" to share their faith. They witness to those with whom they work, and they pray for God to use them in sharing the gospel. My mother, who went to be with the Lord last year, was like that. In fact, when I visited her one week before she died, she asked me to pray two things: "That the Lord will call me home soon, and that He will use me to lead one more soul to Him before I go." She had her chance three days before she died. While serving as a crisis pregnancy hotline counselor (which she often did), a 17-year-old pregnant girl called in desperation. She was phone-patched into my mother's home, where after an hour's conversation she prayed to receive Christ. Not a bad legacy for my mother to leave her children and grandchildren!

THE CROWN OF GLORY

First Peter 5:1,4 tells us about the "elder's crown," or as he calls it, "the crown of glory." There seems to be a special crown for those spiritual elders who share the Word of God. They could be ministers, Sunday school teachers, Child Evangelism teachers, or anyone who teaches the Word of God faithfully to others. Such individuals rarely get adequate rewards in this life, but they certainly will in the life to come.

Now that we have examined these five crowns, it would be good to take a few minutes to analyze which of these crowns you may receive. Don't live such a self-centered, unsurrendered life that you have no crown at all on judgment day. Remember, we are in a race—a long one. Some Christians make good sprinters and serve the Lord well for a few years, but it is a wise servant who always keeps his body under discipline, lives a holy life year after year, wins as many people to Christ as he can, endures persecution when necessary, and teaches the Word of God whenever possible. Such a Christian will not regret this kind of life on judgment day!

The judgment seat of Christ will be an exciting experience of the faithful child of God—which I hope you are. But it will be a miserable "judgment of loss" for those who love the world and the things of this world so much that they never get around to serving the Lord, who paid such a price to save them.

Figure 14 on the next page describes their plight.

> If anyone's work which he has built on it endures, he will receive a reward. If anyone's work is burned, he will suffer loss; but he himself will be saved, yet so as through fire (1 Corinthians 3:14,15).

The judgment seat of Christ precedes His coming to earth to set up His kingdom by a very brief time—perhaps as short as days or even hours. Its purpose is to reward His faithful servants with job assignments during the thousand years of His kingdom. You will serve Christ during that period in direct proportion to the way you have faithfully served Him during this time on earth. If you have been a spectator Christian in this life, you will be one in the next. Your reward earned from this life will determine your opportunity to serve Christ for a thousand years. In the final analysis it is entirely up to you—for a thousand years!

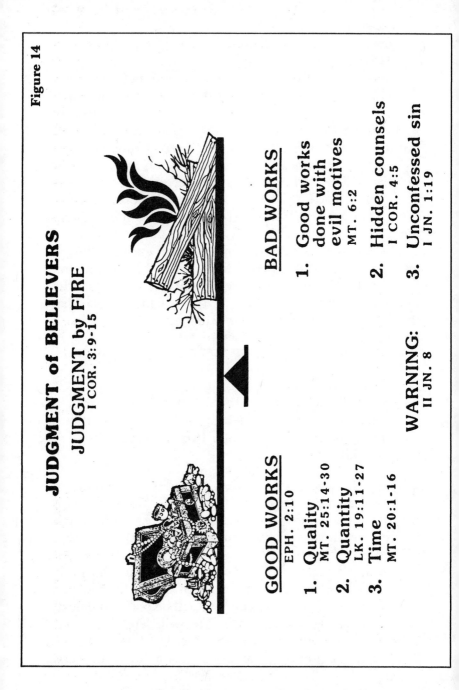

Figure 14

JUDGMENT of BELIEVERS

JUDGMENT by FIRE
I COR. 3:9-15

GOOD WORKS
EPH. 2:10

1. Quality
   MT. 25:14-30
2. Quantity
   LK. 19:11-27
3. Time
   MT. 20:1-16

BAD WORKS

1. Good works
   done with
   evil motives
   MT. 6:2
2. Hidden counsels
   I COR. 4:5
3. Unconfessed sin
   I JN. 1:19

WARNING:
II JN. 8

THE GLORIOUS APPEARING OF CHRIST

The second advent, as it is often called today, refers to that "day of the Lord" when Christ shall come again to this earth in power and great glory to rule and reign personally over this earth. As we have seen, most of the many biblical references to "the second coming" mean the glorious appearing when Christ will come as King of Kings and Lord of Lords, fulfilling the other phase of the prophecies of the Old Testament which state that "the government will be upon His shoulder . . . [and] of the increase of His government and peace there will be no end" (Isaiah 9:6,7).

Our Lord will be the last world emperor. However, as we shall see, His kingdom will be unlike any that ever existed before. It will be a kingdom of peace and prosperity, the curse on the earth will be lifted, and man's inhumanity to man will cease. For the first time since the Garden of Eden, man will love his neighbor as himself.

But before Christ sets up His kingdom, He must come in power and great glory. The next study guide will allow you to study that event for yourself.

$$\boxed{\text{STUDY GUIDE 27}}$$

The Glorious Appearing
Revelation 19

✦

Go back to Study Guide 6 and restudy the passages that describe this event. In one sentence, write a summary of those texts. _____

What precedes the second coming, according to Revelation 19:5-9? _____

_____

_____

Read Revelation 19:11-21 and pick out the five titles for the Lord Jesus Christ.

1) _____

2) _____

3) _____

4) _____

5) _____

Who is the rider on the white horse in verse 11? _____

_____

What is his weapon of war (verse 15)? _____

_____

What does verse 15b mean? _____

_____

How does he slay the multitudes (verse 21)? _____

_____

What happens to the kings of the earth (verses 19-21)? _

_____

What happens to the Beast (verse 20)? _____

_____

What happens to the False Prophet (verse 20)? _____

_____

What happens to Satan (Revelation 20:1-3)? _____

_____

===

✦

SUMMARY

When Christ comes the next time, it will not be to suffer, as He did in His first coming. This time He will come in power and great glory on a white horse, accompanied by the angelic hosts of heaven and His Bride, the church, which He has just purified and judged in preparation for ruling this earth.

All those who hate God will be gathered together against Christ to do war with Him. They will be led by the Antichrist or "the Beast," who is indwelt by Satan himself. With him will be the False Prophet and the Christ-rejecting kings of the earth. They will bring the largest armies of the world ever gathered in what the Bible calls "the war of the great day of God the Almighty," popularly called "the Battle of Armageddon."

But this will be one war where there will be no fighting! The combatants will be prepared to fight, but our Lord's awesome power will consume them in one moment by the word of His mouth—and all those who accepted the mark of the Beast during the tribulation period will be consumed. This will conclude the seven-year tribulation and usher in the kingdom over which Christ will reign. At this time He will judge the nations and decide who will be able to go into the millennial kingdom.

152 ♦ Resurrected Christians

The Judgment of the Nations
Matthew 25:31-46

♦

When does this event occur (verse 31)? _____

_____

Who stands before Christ (verse 32a)? _____

_____

How does He separate the people (verses 32,33)? _____

_____

What is the basis on which He makes this separation (verses
34-40)? _____

_____

_____

Why do some miss the kingdom (verses 41-46)? _____

_____

What happens to these people (verse 46)? _____

_____

Do the people get into the kingdom by faith or by works?

_____

How do you relate this to Ephesians 2:8,9? _____

_____

_____

✦

SUMMARY

When Christ finishes His glorious appearing, there will be only two kinds of people on the earth: 1) the Jews, and 2) those who are good to the Jews (whom Jesus called "My brethren" in Matthew 25:40) during the tribulation period. This latter group also refuse to follow the Antichrist by worshiping him and taking his mark. Instead, they will risk their lives during this time when he targets the Jews for persecution by being good to them and seeking to protect them. All those who accepted "the mark of the Beast" during the tribulation period will be killed at Christ's coming. Those who had accepted the mark of the heavenly Father will have been martyred during the seven-year tribulation. These are called tribulation saints and are described in Revelation 7.

The judgment of the nations is to determine who goes into the kingdom in their natural bodies. In all likelihood it will not be a huge population. It will consist of only two kinds of natural-bodied people—the Jews, and those who at personal risk during the tribulation period defied the Antichrist and reached out to help them.

One important thing to consider here is that this is the only time in the Bible that men are rewarded like this for good works. That is why we know that this parable is not on how to be saved, for no one can earn salvation—even by being good to persecuted Jews. But during the tribulation period, people can gain favor with God and earn the right to go into the millennium in their natural bodies to enjoy and populate the millennial earth during Christ's kingdom by being good to the Jews, and refusing the mark of the Antichrist.

Evidently there will be some people from many countries of the world, probably those in remote areas who helped "His brethren" in the flesh, much as did Christians like Corrie Ten Boom, who defied Hitler during the Holocaust to provide haven to His brethren. People cannot be saved by such deeds, but they can gain entrance into Christ's earthly kingdom.

Such individuals, though unsaved, would undoubtedly be earnest truth-seekers, much like Cornelius in Acts 10 and the Ethiopian eunuch of Acts 8. They will probably respond in faith soon after gaining access to the kingdom and living under our Lord's righteous rulership. It will be at this time that God will fulfill the many prophecies of the Old Testament given to the nation of Israel. He will "create a new heart in them" to obey His will and commit themselves to a lifetime of serving Him. With Satan bound so he cannot tempt the world, the kingdom age with its Edenic or Utopian existence will be unlike any period the world has ever known before.

One thing to notice while we are on this subject: The church does not usher in the kingdom by taking over the governments of the world. The tribulation period will end with few if any Christians on the earth. The Antichrist will be in control, and the earth will be filled with leaders who hate God and His Christ (except for the two types mentioned above). This is why it is necessary for Christ to come in "great power and glory" to wrest control of the world from these evil forces.

VARIOUS VIEWS OF THE KINGDOM

During the 2000-year history of the church there have been three primary views of our Lord's return in relation to the millennial kingdom. Because some in the church today still hold one or the other of these views, you should know something about them. These views are called "premillennial," "postmillennial," and "amillennial."

Premillennialism. This is the oldest of the views and dominated the thinking of the early Christians for the first three centuries. Basically the prefix "pre" means that Christ will come again *before* the kingdom or 1000-year millennium. This has been the interpretation of this book.

Amillennialism. "A" indicates "no," meaning that no literal millennium is expected by those who hold this view. They believe that the spiritual kingdom of Christ has operated simultaneously with the earthly satanic kingdom for 2000 years, and that there will be only one general resurrection (when Christ will separate the saved and lost), followed by heaven. This view was popularized by Augustine in the fourth century, and it became the dominant view of Roman Catholicism (and is to this day). During the Dark Ages, when Christians had little access to the Bible, this view went almost unchallenged. But after the Bible was translated and printed in the fifteenth century so that Christians could study it for themselves, it produced Protestantism, which emphasized many Bible doctrines long forgotten, such as justification by faith. Eventually such Bible study also revived premillennialism.

Postmillennialism. This view holds that Christ will come *after* the earthly kingdom. Proponents believe that we are in (or entering) the kingdom already, that the church is gaining ground on the earth, and that it will become so strong that it will governmentally usher in the era of peace described in prophecy—after which Christ will return.

This view was popularized by the writings of Daniel Whitby (1638-1726), who was a Unitarian, a liberal, and a freethinker. The theory was geared to the evolutionary view of man and the initiation of the industrial revolution. For a while, the future appeared bright. People looked for a Utopian state on earth, a golden age of converted people

156 + *Resurrected Christians*

brought about by the noble efforts of the church, after which Christ would return. However, Whitby's writings on the Godhead were publicly burned and he was denounced as a heretic. Yet his millennial view was keyed to the times, for it expressed what people wanted to hear and initiated a prophetic school of considerable influence.*

Postmillennialism, with its Utopian view of the future, fell on hard times during this century, following two world wars and the unmatched inhumanities of Communism inspired by both the Soviets and Chinese. Because it allegorizes prophecy, this view has not had much acceptance among Bible-believing Christians. In recent years "reconstructionists" and "dominionists" have tried to revive it, but it has made few inroads among those who take a literal view of prophecy. For example, Revelation 20, which six times in six verses indicates that the length of the kingdom age will be "one thousand years," must be taken either literally or figuratively. If you take it literally you are probably a premillennialist. If you take it symbolically you are probably either a postmillennialist or amillennialist. (Not all who hold a postmillennial view are liberals. Some fine Christians who take the rest of the Bible literally take prophecy symbolically, although it is this writer's belief that doing so creates more problems than it solves. Figure 15 [page 158] should be studied in the light of these three views.)

Premillennialism, which has been under a small but noisy attack today by some of the above-mentioned postmillennialists, traces its roots back to the apostles Paul (2 Thessalonians 2:1-12) and John (Revelation) as well as most of the early church fathers. This view dropped out of sight during the Dark Ages (dark because the Bible was kept in monasteries and museums and not studied by the people).

---

* Adapted from Gerald B. Stanton, *Why I Am a Premillennialist* (private publication, 1976), p. 4.

Later, as Bibles began to be printed and distributed during the sixteenth and seventeenth centuries, Christians began studying God's Word for themselves, which led to the revival of premillennialism. It was widely popularized by John Darby, the founder of the Brethren movement, a church deeply committed to Bible study during the middle of the nineteenth century. In the twentieth century premillennialism became the dominant view of the Bible-believing church through the writings of C.I. Scofield (author of the Scofield Bible notes) as well as through the Fundamentalist movement of the 1920's and 30's and the teachings of Dallas Theological Seminary (and certain other schools). Premillennialism does not answer every complex question of prophecy, but for those who try to interpret the Scriptures literally, it answers more questions than any other view of prophecy.

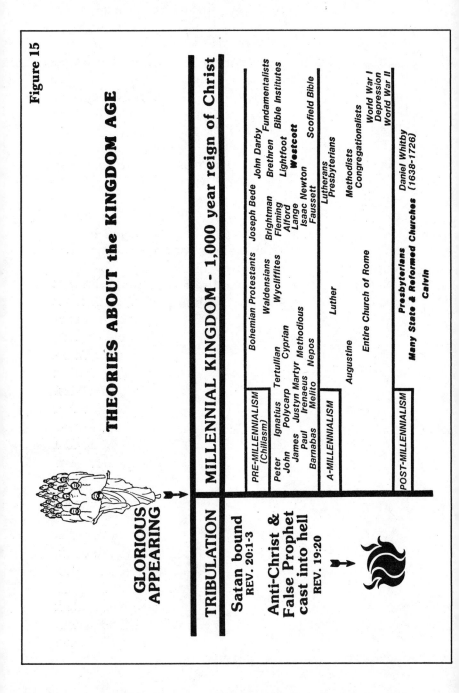

Figure 15

THEORIES ABOUT the KINGDOM AGE

CHAPTER 14

The Coming Kingdom of Christ

♦

One thing that both Jews and Christians agree on is that someday their Messiah is going to come to this earth to set up His kingdom that shall rule the earth. It will be a time of peace, blessing and joy that will be interrupted only briefly at the end, before eternity or "Heaven" is ushered in. There is, of course, great disagreement on the identity of that Messiah. Christians believe that Jesus Christ is that Messiah, and that He will return to set up His kingdom and that they will rule it with Him. Jews, on the other hand, believe that an unknown Jew will yet come as Messiah to set up that kingdom. What is interesting is that even though most Jews do not know it, the requirements of their Messiah make Him identical to Jesus Christ! But both groups agree that when Messiah comes He will reign over this earth.

There are far too many passages in the Bible that predict a future kingdom than we could possibly study in this book. We can, however, select some of the most significant passages. Again, rather than prejudice you to accept my position before you formulate your own, I will assign you select passages to study so you can come to your own conclusions. Then in the summary I will give my commentary. This can be a most interesting and inspiring study.

STUDY GUIDE 29

The Coming Kingdom of Christ

✦

Isaiah 9:6,7 is one of those passages that merge the first and second comings of Christ into one prophecy. What do these verses teach about His first coming? _____

_____

Were you surprised to find that most of this passage relates to the second coming? _____

Who will bear the weight of the government (verse 6a)?

_____

Give the five titles for Christ in verse 6.

1) _____

2) _____

3) _____

4) _____

5) _____

Describe how His kingdom will flourish (verse 7). _____

_____

What is meant by the term "throne of David"? _____

_____

How long will it last? _____

List three words that describe His kingdom.

1) _____
2) _____
3) _____

Who guarantees it (verse 7c)? _____

STUDY GUIDE 30

The Kingdom in the Old Testament

✦

Daniel 2:31-35 contains a most important prophecy given by God to a pagan king, a man who may have been the most absolute ruler in the history of the world. Read and describe it in your own words.

_____

_____

_____

_____

Daniel 2:37-45 gives God's interpretation through Daniel to the above vision. Study it carefully and describe it.

_____

_____

_____

_____

_____

Who sets up the Rock Kingdom? _____

Who is the "Rock"? _____

Isaiah 61:1-11 is the passage which our Lord quoted in the synagogue of Nazareth. We saw how He claimed that His first coming fulfilled verses 1 through 2a (Luke 4:21). Study these 11 verses and list briefly seven characteristics of the future kingdom.

1) _____

2) _____

3) _____

4) _____

5) _____

6) _____

7) _____

By any stretch of the imagination could this ever have occurred in past history? _____

STUDY GUIDE 31

Conditions of the Future Kingdom
Isaiah 65:13-25

✦

List five things in Isaiah 65:19-23 that will not exist in this glorious kingdom.

1) _____

2) _____

3) _____

4) _____

5) _____

How old are children (verse 20b)? _____

Who dies at that age (verse 20c)? _____

How permanent and prosperous will the kingdom be (verses 21-23)? _____

_____

_____

_____

What does verse 24 suggest? _____

_____

Describe verse 25 conditions. _____

_____

_____

_____

✦

THE TWO PHASES OF THE KINGDOM IN THE NEW TESTAMENT

There are almost 200 references to the kingdom in the New Testament, but unlike the Old Testament, most of them (except for those in the book of Revelation) have to do with the *spiritual* phase of the kingdom. To save you confusion, I will explain those two phases.

The *spiritual* phase of the kingdom is what our Lord came to establish in His first coming. He told Pilate that He was a King, but that His kingdom "was not of this world." He also said that a person must be "born again" to get into His kingdom. John the Baptist said that people had to "repent" to get into the kingdom of God. We have already studied Paul's assertion that "flesh and blood cannot inherit the kingdom of God." So the Lord first of all established a spiritual kingdom into which people are born by faith in Christ's death, burial, and resurrection. Such individuals are then entitled to enter the *literal* kingdom of God on this earth when Christ comes physically to set it up.

That is why any attempt to establish the kingdom of God on earth before Christ comes is doomed to failure. The task of the church today is not "kingdom-building." Instead, it is to advance the spiritual kingdom by preaching the gospel around the world. This does not mean that Christians who are members of that spiritual kingdom by faith in Christ do not have a responsibility to be both "salt" and "light" during this present age. Christians are to be salt in that they are a morally savoring influence on society by participating as good citizens in voting, running for office, and serving both their God and their country as good stewards.

Some do this as schoolteachers, ministers, Christian attorneys, authors, artists, or movie producers, and others by running for public office as school board members, city councilmen, congressmen, senators, etc. All responsible "salty citizens" will be careful to vote on election day to keep anti-Christians from ruling over us and limiting our freedom to fulfill our primary task, which is to be the light of the world in fulfillment of the Great Commission. Hopefully, in the closing years of the church age, Christians will be more faithful in these dual challenges than was Israel in the Old Testament.

The kingdom which our Lord will set up when He comes will be made up of three kinds of people, as we saw in the preceding chapter: 1) Jews who survive the tribulation, in their natural bodies; 2) Gentiles who were good to the Jews, in their natural bodies; and 3) the resurrected saints of all ages in their resurrected bodies.

Except for Revelation 20, most of the New Testament passages have to do with the spiritual phase of the kingdom, which is often used interchangeably with the church. Examine Matthew 16:16-19, where our Lord told Peter He would "build My church" on the rock of Peter's testimony (that Christ was "the Son of the living God"). He then promised to give Peter "the keys of the kingdom of heaven" ("The kingdom of God" and "the kingdom of heaven" are often used interchangeably—compare Matthew 13 and Mark 4). "The kingdom of God" in the New Testament usually refers to the true church, that body of believers who enter the church by faith in Christ and then spend the rest of their lives sharing that faith so others can also become members of "His body, the church." The literal physical kingdom is yet future and is best described in the Old

Testament and Revelation 20. It will be set up when Christ returns in power, because He alone has the power to set it up.

STUDY GUIDE 32

Conditions During Christ's Kingdom

✦

What happens to Satan at the beginning of Christ's kingdom (Revelation 20:1-3)? _____

_____

What effect will that have on the earth? _____

_____

Why is Satan bound during the kingdom (verse 3b)? ___

_____

What effect will that have on faith and people coming to Christ? _____

_____

_____

Who will get into this kingdom according to verse 4? ___

_____

What will those people do during the kingdom? _____

_____

How long will the kingdom last? _____

How many times is the duration of the kingdom mentioned in verses 2-7? _____

Why is that important? _____

What does verse 6 say the resurrected saints will do during the kingdom? _____

Why is Satan released at the end of the kingdom (verses 7,8)? _____

_____

How successful will he be (verses 8,9)? _____

_____

Then what happens to Satan (verse 10)? _____

_____

Who is already there? _____

What does that suggest about eternal suffering? _____

_____

How long will they suffer? _____

Then what happens (verses 11-15)? _____

✦

KINGDOM SUMMARY

The coming literal kingdom of Christ to this earth will be the most blessed time this world has known since the Garden of Eden. In fact, many Edenic features will characterize it. All those who rebel against God will be gone. Satan will be bound literally so he cannot tempt man, which accounts for how Christ will be able to enforce righteousness. Of course, together with His holy angels, He will have the church in their new resurrected bodies to help Him enforce His reign of righteousness. No doubt it will be illegal for pornographers, criminals, and others who traditionally corrupt society to ply their evil trades.

The coming kingdom will be a time of unprecedented prosperity, when everyone will have his own home. The curse on the earth will be lifted and the ground will bear incredible harvests. Cheating and war will be nonexistent, so people will enjoy the fruits of their labors.

Isaiah 65 indicates that longevity will be increased to almost what it was prior to the flood, when people lived to almost 1000 years of age. At least that will be the case for believers, who will live from the time of their birth until the end of the kingdom. Verse 20 indicates that a person will be considered still a child at 100 years of age.

A TIME OF FAITH

The millennial kingdom will be a time of faith, when the majority of the population will become believers. We see that in several passages. Christ will be in charge, so there won't be immoral or other forms of destructive TV programming or pornography to blind men's minds to the gospel. Body-damaging substances will not be available, so people will not have their minds so fogged that they cannot fairly appraise the truths of Scripture; Satan will be bound so he cannot "blind their eyes." The university chairs of learning will not be dominated by atheists set to destroy the minds of youth. Instead, all education will start from the premise "In the beginning GOD!" In such an academic climate, young people will be more open to the claims of God and Christ on their lives. Even art forms will glorify Christ during the kingdom. Jeremiah 31:31-34 indicates that everyone will be so acquainted with the gospel that no one will need to share it with his neighbor.

Isaiah 65:20 indicates that unbelievers will die "being 100 years old." That suggests enormous consequences for the high percentage of believers living at that time, for it indicates that only Christians will live beyond their hundredth birthday. Evidently God will give people 100 years to decide about Christ. If they accept Him, they are permitted to live on for the rest of the kingdom period. But no sinner will survive his hundredth birthday. That fact alone would mean that only Christians will be alive to propagate and raise children after they are 100 years old. From this fact, along with the ideal cultural environment we saw in the above paragraph, it is probable that as high as 80 or more percent of the population will be saved during that age.

A REBELLIOUS YOUTH MOVEMENT

But in spite of all the ideal conditions arranged by God to attract a maximum number of people to accept His free salvation by receiving His Son, millions will rebel at the end of the thousand-year kingdom, for Revelation 20 indicates that at the end of the thousand years Satan will be loosed from the bottomless pit to go out "to deceive the nations"—that is, to tempt them to rebel against God. The reason for this tempting is so that all the people living on the earth who are still unsaved will be forced to make a decision about whether they will receive Christ before God establishes the eternal order. We have already seen that these will be people under 100 years of age, according to Isaiah 65:20, for only believers will live past their hundredth birthday.

The sad part of this whole story is that even after living for almost a hundred years under the righteous reign of Christ, there will still be a multitude "whose number is as the sand of the sea" who will rebel against God when given the opportunity. Among other things, this suggests that it isn't entirely Satan's fault that people reject faith in Christ, but results from the rebellion of their own will. Satan coming on the scene at this point only brings to the surface the rebellion of many hearts who, like many Jews of our Lord's day, "willed not to come" to Him that they might have eternal life (John 5:40).

The End of Satan

Revelation 20:10 says, "And the devil, who deceived them, was cast into the lake of fire and brimstone, where the beast and the false prophet are. And they will be tormented day and night forever and ever." The ability of living creatures to suffer indefinitely in the lake of fire is seen in the fact that the Beast (or Antichrist) and the False Prophet are men. They are thrown into the lake of fire at the beginning of the thousand-year kingdom (Revelation 19:20), yet they are spoken of in the present tense in Revelation 20:10, indicating that they are still there. It is into this lake of fire that Satan is cast. He, the Antichrist, the False Prophet, and all those from every age in history who rejected God's free offer of salvation through faith in Christ "will be tormented day and night forever and ever." That is the strongest word structure in the Bible for eternity!

The Two Stages of the First Resurrection

The Bible is a book of life—eternal life. Yet we are faced every day with the reality of death, from the death of babies to the death of the oldest people in our society. The only way to correlate these two contrasting states of life and death is to remember that *all the dead will eventually be resurrected.* We have already seen that our Lord's bodily resurrection guarantees the Christian's eventual resurrection. It is important to realize that there are *two resurrections,* called in Scripture 1) "the first resurrection" (also called "the resurrection unto life") and 2) "the second resurrection" (which is the same as "the resurrection of damnation" or judgment). Daniel, the great Old Testament prophet, associated both of these resurrections with the time of the end, when "there shall be a time of trouble, such as never was since there was a nation...." Then he added, "Many of those who sleep in the dust of the earth shall awake, some to everlasting life, some to shame and everlasting contempt" (Daniel 12:1,2).

The first resurrection is not a single event, but takes place in two stages which are separated by at least seven years.

The first stage of the first resurrection is the rapture of the church, which as we have already seen includes both living and dead Christians. When the Lord shouts for His church from heaven, He will resurrect the dead in Christ (all those who "sleep in Jesus"). Then "we who are alive and remain shall be caught up together with them in the clouds to meet the Lord in the air. And thus we shall always be with the Lord" (1 Thessalonians 4:17). Very simply, this means that all those who have received Jesus Christ as their personal Savior, whether living or dead at the time He comes in the air to rapture His church, will be a part of this first stage of the first resurrection. The most comforting part of all is the promise that no matter what happens after that, we will "always be with the Lord."

But what many people don't seem to realize is that there are *two stages* of the first resurrection. After the first stage, millions of people will yet call upon the name of the Lord and be saved, principally during the seven-year tribulation period. Then, when our Lord comes to this earth to set up

His thousand-year kingdom of righteousness, He will resurrect the rest of the believers. In the words of the prophet
John:

> And I saw thrones, and they [the saints] sat on
> them, and judgment was given to them. And I saw
> the souls of those who had been beheaded for
> their witness to Jesus and for the word of God,
> who had not worshiped the beast or his image,
> and had not received his mark on their foreheads
> or on their hands. And they lived and reigned
> with Christ for a thousand years (Revelation 20:4).

Then he writes:

> But the rest of the dead [the unbelievers] did
> not live again until the thousand years were fin-
> ished. This is the first resurrection. Blessed and
> holy is he who has part in the first resurrection.
> Over such the second death [eternal condemna-
> tion] has no power, but they will be priests of God
> and of Christ, and will reign with Him a thousand
> years (Revelation 20:5,6).

The second stage of the first resurrection will probably
include (according to Psalm 50:1-6) all the Old Testament
saints who went to their graves with faith in God and His
future sacrifice for their sin, plus the tribulation saints,
most of whom will be martyrs because they refused to
worship the Antichrist. These shall "be priests," and,
like Christians raised at the rapture and judged for their
works as believers, "they will reign with Him a thousand
years."

The "rest of the dead," or all the unbelievers who lived
from the days of Adam and Eve until Christ comes to set up
His kingdom, will not be raised until the end of that kingdom age, which comes just before eternity. That is called

"the second resurrection." It is a resurrection of the lost to judgment and then to eternal separation from God. But before we can examine that issue, we must back up slightly and find out where they are now.

CHAPTER 15

Where the Dead Are Now

✦

The most traumatic event in my life was my father's death three weeks before my tenth birthday. Until a person has gone through the tragedy of the loss of a close loved one, he rarely thinks about death. We tend to assume that life goes on forever, but real death destroys those illusions and creates questions that we have never before contemplated.

In my case, the first question I asked my mother was, "Where is Dad now?" That is probably the most commonly asked question under those circumstances, and not only by children. Everyone is curious about life in the afterlife. As far back as we can go in history, man has asked Job's classic question: "If a man die, shall he live again?" Life is so precious to human beings that the desire to live on in some future state is almost universal. Library shelves are filled with books on the subject, and practically every religion known to man offers some kind of teaching on the subject.

Looking back, I detect something interesting about my childhood reaction to my father's death that is common to many people. At no time did I consider the possibility that he had ceased to exist, for my question indicated my assurance that he, the real person, was still alive somewhere. I just didn't know where. Fortunately for me (and certainly my father), my parents had become Christians six years before he died. As I discovered later, that was the most important decision he ever made, for it determined where he spent his afterlife.

Due to that boyhood experience of death, I have studied the subject in great detail. My library is stocked with collections of books and articles on the subject from all over the world. It is my considered opinion that no one will be accurately informed on death until he studies the Bible's teaching and interprets all other writings in the light of it.

The Bible is a book of life, not of death. Yet like any book of history, it has to include the fact that men and women die. But the Bible also points out that humans can make arrangements while they live to enjoy eternal life in the next world. Although the Bible focuses extensively upon eternal and physical *life*, it also treats the subject of death many times. The 66 books of the Bible have much to say about death and the future life, since God meant for man to know the truth. He knew that ignorance would arouse some of man's greatest fears. Yet when an individual knows God personally and is aware of what Scripture teaches about the afterlife, he is not afraid of death.

To get a comprehensive picture of God's presentation about death, we must turn to several books of the Bible and consider various references in the light of others, thereby building a composite description. If you are fascinated by the subject of life in the afterlife, you will find our study most rewarding.

THE WORLD OF THE DEAD

The 39 books of the Old Testament refer to the world of

the dead 65 times as "sheol." The word may be translated as "the grave," "hell," or "death." Sheol must not be confused with "the pit" or "the lake of fire," for sheol is the place of all those who have departed this life, both believers and unbelievers. The New Testament word for this world of the dead is "hades" (appearing 42 times). It is important to note that "sheol" and "hades" are not really "hell," as the King James version translates it. The Hebrew word "sheol" and the Greek word "hades" both refer to the same temporary place, whereas "hell" is a permanent place which lasts forever.

"Tartarus," a word that occurs only once in the entire Bible (2 Peter 2:4), is defined by Bible scholars as "the deepest abyss of hades." Admittedly we don't know much about that deep abyss, except that, as part of hades, it too is probably temporary.

"Gehenna" is the New Testament word for the permanent place of the dead, used by Jesus Christ Himself 11 times. James also used it (James 3:6). Of Hebrew origin from "valley" and "Hinnom," the word refers to the Valley of Hinnom, just outside Jerusalem, where the refuse of the city was dumped. It was characteristic of this valley that a fire was continually burning there. Many Bible scholars see this as a perfect characterization of hell—a place where "the fire is not quenched" (Mark 9:48), or the "lake of fire" (Revelation 20:14), referring to the final place of dead souls who have rejected God.

The King James version of the Bible translates all of these words—sheol, hades, gehenna, or Tartarus the same: "hell." This leads to the confusing idea that they refer to the same place, when in fact they do not. Several modern versions have clearly distinguished among these words. The New American Standard version, for example, calls the temporary places "sheol" or "hades," and the final place of the dead "hell."

The Old Testament Teaching on Sheol

✦

The following are some of the outstanding Old Testament verses on the state of those who have died. After the Scripture reference write in what you think the verse teaches about it.

Proverbs 9:18: _____

Psalm 86:13: _____

Psalm 9:17: _____

Genesis 44:29: _____

Psalm 88:3: _____

Psalm 89:48: _____

Deuteronomy 32:22: _____

Song of Solomon 8:6: _____

Ecclesiastes 9:10: _____

Ezekiel 32:21: _____

Isaiah 14:9,10: _____

Psalm 49:15: _____

Study your answers carefully and write a synopsis of what the Old Testament teaches about life after death. Be careful not to inject anything you already know from the New Testament.

_____

_____

_____

_____

_____

=======================

STUDY GUIDE 34

The New Testament Teaching on Destiny After Death
Luke 16:19-31

✦

=======================

The New Testament presumes a knowledge of the Old Testament's teachings on the afterlife. But the best teaching in it came from the greatest of all sources—the creator Himself, the Lord Jesus Christ.

Read Luke 16:19-31 carefully. Did Jesus call this a parable?

_____

Describe the unnamed man of the story in verse 19, and tell what happened to him. _____

_____

Describe Lazarus and tell what happened to him.

_____

_____

Describe what happened to both of them immediately after
death (verses 22-24). _____

_____

Note their contrasting lifestyles and contrasting eternities
(verses 25,26). _____

_____

What place separates the two states of the dead (verse 26)?

_____

Describe the rich man's request in verses 27,28. _____

_____

Why did Abraham refuse it (verse 29)? _____

_____

What did the rich man recognize that his brothers needed
to do in order to avoid that place (verse 30)? _____

_____

How powerful a witness did Abraham think the Word of
God is (verse 31)? _____

_____

✦

Study Figure 16, Where the Dead Are Now, on the next page before reading the summary. See if you can locate the events you have just studied. Then examine this chart as you read the summary.

SUMMARY

It is important to note that this story is not a parable, but the record of a specific experience. Characters in parables are not given definite names but are identified as "a certain man," "a man," "a householder," etc. This story lists names—Abraham and Lazarus—as Jesus relates the factual record of two men who lived and died (possibly just prior to the narration of the story). They both went to hades, but not to the same part. Figure 16 (on the next page) will clarify our Lord's teaching on this subject and will serve as a basic guide to all the future events discussed in this book.

It appears from this passage that hades is composed of three compartments: "Abraham's bosom," "the great gulf fixed," and "the place of torment."

The most desirable compartment in hades, picturesquely called "Abraham's bosom" or "paradise," is a place of comfort. In Luke 16:25 Abraham says of Lazarus, "Now he is comforted." This would be the paradise of the Old Testament to which the souls of the righteous dead went immediately after death. We can rightly assume that, like Lazarus, they were carried by the angels to this place of comfort. It is also a place of companionship for Lazarus, since he has the joy of fellowship with Abraham. No matter how he was treated on the earth, he now holds an enviable position by the side of Abraham. This, of course, introduces a wonderful possibility of fellowship with all the other saints of God gone on before: Elijah, Moses, David, and many others.

Very few details are given about the second compartment, the "great gulf fixed," but we know that it is an

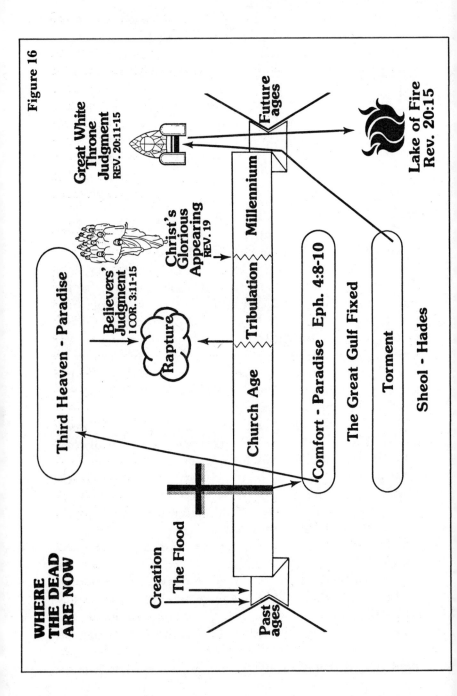

Figure 16

impassable gulf over which men may look and converse but not cross. God designed it "so that those who want to pass from here to you cannot, nor can those from there pass to us." It is evidently a chasm that separates the believers and unbelievers in the next life. Once a person dies, he is confined to one side or the other—comfort or torment. (Some Bible teachers also believe that this great gulf has no bottom to it, and that it could well be the "bottomless pit" of Revelation 20:3 into which the devil is cast at the glorious appearing of the Lord Jesus Christ.)

More details are given about the "place of torment" than the other compartments. The Lord Jesus was clearly interested in warning people about this place in order to keep them from going there. The rich man called hades a *place* of torments, indicating that it is a real place and not merely a state of existence, as some people would like to believe. Luke 16:22 tells us that "the rich man also died and was buried"; verse 23 begins, "And being in torments in hades, he lifted up his eyes." There seems to be no intermediate state, for the unbeliever goes immediately to the place of torment. Verse 23 also suggests that a person is conscious of what he missed, for it states, "He lifted up his eyes and saw Abraham afar off, and Lazarus in his bosom." This indicates that one of the horrible tortures of hades will be to look across the great gulf fixed and view the comforts and blessings of those who are believers and are now comforted The unbeliever will constantly be reminded of what he has missed due to his rejection of God.

It is impossible to be absolutely certain of the exact geographical location of sheol-hades. Some think it is in the heart of the earth, while others think it lies in some undesignated spot in the universe. The Bible refers to it as "down" in Numbers 16:33, which might be responsible for the supposition that it is in the heart of the earth. Actually, the geographical location is not important. It is crucially important, however, that this awful place of torment be avoided.

ESCAPE FROM SHEOL-HADES

One of the many outstanding changes brought about by the death, burial, and resurrection of Jesus Christ is that the believer has escaped from sheol-hades. Psalm 16:10, as quoted by Peter in Acts 2:25-31, establishes the fact that Jesus Christ is not in sheol-hades today. The location of hades is spoken of as "down," but we find in Acts 1:9,10 that the Lord Jesus was "taken up, and a cloud received Him out of their sight. And while they looked steadfastly toward heaven as He went up...." Second Corinthians 5:8 tells us, "We are confident, yes, well-pleased rather to be absent from the body and to be present with the Lord." In other words, the believer at death does not go to sheol-hades, but is present with the Lord, who is not in sheol-hades because He dwells in heaven. In fact, the Scriptures teach that the Lord Jesus is presently "standing at the right hand of God" (Acts 7:55). Consequently, when a present-day believer (or any Christian during the church age) dies, he no longer goes to sheol-hades, but his soul proceeds immediately to heaven to be with his Savior, Jesus Christ.

One question naturally confronts us: "When did this change take place?" We know that the Lord Jesus went to paradise, for in Luke 23:43 He told the thief on the cross who cried out for salvation, "Today you will be with Me in Paradise." So we know that Jesus went directly from the cross into the paradise section of sheol-hades. Now look at Ephesians 4:8-10. This passage reveals that paradise is no longer located in hades, but was taken by Christ up into heaven. This would indicate that the believer now goes to heaven, where he is joined with the Old and New Testament departed saints, leaving the former paradise section of hades an empty compartment. It is also very possible that at this time the Lord Jesus snatched the keys of hades and death from the hand of Satan, for we see in Revelation 1:18 that He now holds them

You are probably wondering why the Old Testament saints were directed to the place of comfort or paradise in the first place. Why couldn't Daniel, David, Abraham, and all those great men and women of God go directly to heaven? After all, they believed in God while they lived. The answer is found in the inadequacy of the covering of their sins. In the Old Testament, sins were temporarily covered by the blood of a "lamb without blemish or without spot." But an animal's blood was not sufficient to permanently cleanse their sins (Hebrews 9:9,10). Sacrifice was an exercise of obedience, showing their faith that God would someday provide permanent cleansing from sin through the sacrifice of His Son.

When our Lord cried from the cross, "It is finished," He meant that the final sacrifice for man's sin was paid. God in human flesh could accomplish what no animal sacrifice could ever do—atone for the sins of the whole world. After releasing His soul, Jesus descended into hades and led all the Old Testament believers, held captive until sin was finally atoned for, up into heaven, where they are presently with Him.

THE SOULISH STATE

We need to be careful not to confuse the present conscious state of the dead with the future resurrected state of the dead. The latter is described by Paul in 1 Corinthians 15, where he speaks of the rapture at which "we shall all be changed." Verses 52 and 53 tell us that at the last trumpet the dead "will be raised incorruptible, and we shall be changed. For this corruptible must put on incorruption, and this mortal must put on immortality." So far the believer has not yet received his incorruptible resurrected body. That body will be described in detail in the next chapter, but for now, remember that it is distinctly different from the present *temporary* state of the dead.

The best term I know to describe this state is "soulish." (Some call it a "soul-spirit" state, but I hesitate to use "spirit" because it is often confused with apparitions or spiritism.) The "soulish state" describes the present condition of the dead. We have already noted that it was described by our Lord in Luke 16:19-31 as a condition of life that is quite different from that of our physical life. It is conscious and recognizable; it can converse and be comforted or tormented. Earthly events are remembered, and those who go to torment may not pass over into comfort. The Old Testament believers, as we have seen, have been taken by Christ up into paradise, where they have been joined by the souls of Christians at death ever since the first century. The soulish state is both conscious and immediate upon death.

NO LIMBO OR PURGATORY

The soulish state should not be confused with "purgatory" or "limbo," which are not a product of the Word of God but a concept of the imagination of man. Purgatory is said to be a place where men go to do penance or suffer for the sins they have committed in this world in order to purify them for a better afterlife. The startling difference between the biblical presentation of the present state of the dead and this false teaching is that there is no indication whatever in the Bible that those in the torment section of sheol-hades or those in heaven will ever be anywhere but where they are for all eternity. We have already learned that anyone in the place of torment will never bridge the great gulf fixed and gain paradise. On the contrary, all those who are presently in torment will eventually be cast into the lake of fire. People are sent from this life into the place of torment because they have not accepted Jesus Christ and because their names are not written in the book of life (Revelation 20:12-15).

The suggestion that those in torment today will be granted a later opportunity to be saved contradicts Isaiah 38:18, which says, "For Sheol cannot thank You, death cannot praise You; those who go down to the pit cannot hope for Your truth." The place of torment is essentially a place of suffering and is void of the teaching of truth. Therefore those who enter that place cannot hope for escape. This is tragically true, but the tragedy does not lessen the truth.

THE WAY TO HADES

The way to hades is the way of neglect. The Bible tells us, "How shall we escape if we neglect so great salvation?" A person winds up in hades not simply because he is rich or poor, or because he is a murderer, a whoremonger, or a thief. A man is sent to hades because he is an *unbeliever*— because he has never accepted Jesus Christ as his own Savior. According to John 3:18, "He who believes in Him is not condemned; but he who does not believe is condemned already, because he has not believed in the name of the only begotten Son of God."

Note that both those who go to paradise and those who end up in hades are sinners. The latter die in their sins, while those who reside in paradise were forgiven of their sins sometime during their earthly life. Jesus Himself gave us clear directions on how to obtain admittance to this glorious place when He said, "I am the way, the truth, and the life. No one comes to the Father except through Me" (John 14:6). Only by Jesus Christ can we gain access to the Father. Inasmuch as the Father is in heaven (where paradise is located), it follows that only by Jesus Christ do we have access to heaven. All of us deserve to go to hell (Romans 3:23; 6:23). and only through faith in the Lord Jesus Christ and His finished work on Calvary's cross can we escape hades and hell. John 1:12 says, "But as many as received Him, to them He gave the right to become children of God, even to those that believe in His name."

THE MESSAGE OF SHEOL

The message of sheol-hades can be put into one word, found in Luke 16:30. The rich man in hades pleaded with Abraham to send Lazarus back to life to warn the rich man's five brethren. What was it that the rich man anxiously wished Lazarus to tell his brothers to do? The answer appears in verse 30: *repent.* He said, "If one goes to them from the dead, they will repent."

If it were possible for a departed soul to return from hades to give one last message to his living loved ones, it would be the same message which the rich man wanted for his brothers—REPENT so that you might avoid this awful place. The greatest tragedy in the world is not that Jesus Christ was crucified on the cross, but that men and women have heard the message of His death to save them from hades and hell but have rejected it, refusing to repent and believe on Him. In spite of the fact that He has died for them, they will spend eternity in torment. To activate the eternal effects of God's forgiveness of sins through the death of His son, a person must call on the name of the Lord and be saved (Romans 10:13). There is no other way—and no second chance.

CHAPTER 16

The Great White Throne Judgment

✦

Written intuitively on the table of every man's heart is the knowledge that one day he will be ushered into God's presence in order to give an account of himself. One of the reasons that many agnostics, humanists, and unbelievers refuse to acknowledge the existence of God is that they are subconsciously afraid of one day facing Him at the judgment. Unfortunately for them, disbelief does not negate the fact of judgment, for the Bible is abundantly clear that after death comes judgment: "It is appointed for men to die once, but after this the judgment" (Hebrews 9:27).

The fact of judgment in the afterlife is not a teaching unique to Christianity; it was taught clearly in the Old Testament. The most frequent mention of this event came from the lips of Jesus Christ, who one day will be the Judge before whom men and women will stand (John 5:22). For a sample of our Lord's teaching on this subject, see Matthew 13:37-43. The most graphic description of that ultimate judgment day when all unsaved people will stand before Him is called "the great white throne judgment" (Revelation 20:11-15). It is awesome to contemplate!

STUDY GUIDE 35

The Great White Throne Judgment

✦

Read Revelation 20:11-15 carefully.

Describe "the dead" of verse 12. (See also 1 Timothy 5:6.)

_____

Name the two kinds of books in verse 12. _____

_____

Why are the books of "works" used (verse 13)? _____

_____

Where do these people come from? _____

_____

Describe the "second death" (verse 14). _____

_____

Look up the following verses and list each title for the book and describe it.

Psalm 69:28: _____

Revelation 13:8: _____

Exodus 32:33: _____

Revelation 3:5: _____

Revelation 21:27: _____

Revelation 22:19: _____

Are these books different? _____

Describe them: _____

_____

_____

What keeps a person from being cast into the lake of fire (Revelation 20:15)? _____

The following Scriptures give us information about the lake of fire. Describe it. _____

_____

Revelation 20:14,15: _____

Revelation 21:8: _____

Mark 9:43: _____

✦

THE TIME OF THIS JUDGMENT

The great white throne judgment occurs at the end of the millennial kingdom, after Satan has led his insurrection but failed. Satan, the Beast, and the False Prophet have already been thrown into the lake of fire. As you look at Figure 16 in the previous chapter, you find this judgment located at the extreme end of the time line, just before the beginning of the ages to come. These ages are called "the new heaven and the new earth" and are predicted in Revelation chapters 21 and 22. The last event, then, just before the heaven that Jesus promised to prepare, is this great white throne judgment.

On a flight from Salt Lake City to San Francisco I was seated next to a salesman who claimed he had never read a Bible. The closest he had ever been to church in his life was to drop off his daughter every other week for Sunday school on his way to the golf course. I asked him if he would submit to an experiment, to which he agreed. Many people say the Bible is a difficult book to understand, particularly the book of Revelation. Turning to Revelation 20:11-19, I handed him my Bible with only a brief instruction: "This is a prophecy about a future event." I waited as he read. His cheerful mood changed abruptly, and soon he exclaimed, "If that's true, I'd better get right with God!"

That salesman put into words the main reason God has given us so much information about the afterlife judgment that awaits all those who reject or neglect God. As an aid to the following comments on this awesome passage in Revelation, we shall examine the details on the next few pages very carefully. Figure 17 is an artist's concept of that event. Please compare it with the description as we proceed.

We have already seen in Acts 17:30,31 that God will judge the world by "the Man whom He has ordained." We may well ask, whom has He ordained? The answer appears in the latter part of the verse: whom He has "raised from the dead." The Lord Jesus Christ is the only Person in world history who can match this description. He is the only One who could judge the world "in righteousness," for only He is "without sin" (1 Peter 2:22).

John 5:22 confirms Christ's identity as the Judge, since Jesus said "The Father judges no one, but has committed all judgment to the Son." Therefore we come to the irrefutable conclusion that the Judge who sits on the great white throne

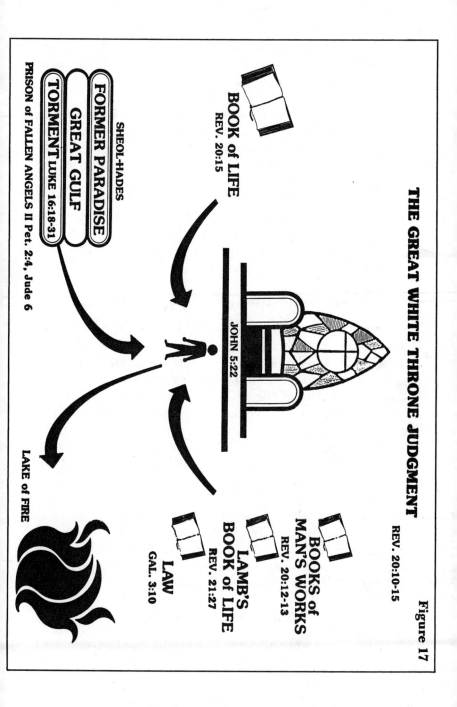

THE GREAT WHITE THRONE JUDGMENT

REV. 20:10-15

Figure 17

BOOK of LIFE
REV. 20:15

JOHN 5:22

BOOKS of
MAN'S WORKS
REV. 20:12-13

LAMB'S
BOOK of LIFE
REV. 21:27

LAW
GAL. 3:10

SHEOL-HADES

FORMER PARADISE

GREAT GULF

TORMENT LUKE 16:19-31

PRISON of FALLEN ANGELS II Pet. 2:4, Jude 6

LAKE of FIRE

is none other than the Lord Jesus Christ Himself. The very Person who was rejected and scorned by men will ultimately sit in judgment on them. That is a very sobering thought!

One imposing feature of Christ being the Judge is that even on this earth in His human body He had the incredible ability to look at a person and know him intimately. You can be sure no individual will be able to hide himself from the Savior's penetrating eye on judgment day! As the Bible says, "There is no creature hidden from His sight, but all things are naked and open to the eyes of Him to whom we must give account" (Hebrews 4:13). We also read, "There is nothing covered that will not be revealed, and hidden that will not be known" (Matthew 10:26).

WHO APPEARS AT THIS JUDGMENT?

Now that we have verified the identity of the Judge, we may ask about the identity of those to be judged. John reports in Revelation 20:12, "I saw the dead, small and great, standing before God." It is significant to note that all those who stand at the great white throne judgment are "the dead"—dead in trespasses and sins because of their rejection of Jesus Christ. Note that the dead are referred to as "small and great." God, who is no respecter of persons, judges fairly without regard to status, whether intellectual, physical, financial, or positional.

Whether their ashes are in the grave, in a mausoleum, on the earth, or in the sea, God will resurrect His creatures to their original bodies, souls, and spirits. Their remains will be resurrected and united with the soul and spirit as they come up out of the place of torment, and in this resurrected form they will stand before the throne.

THE VARIOUS BOOKS OF JUDGMENT

"And books were opened.... And the dead were judged according to their works, by the things which were written in the books" (Revelation 20:12). Evidently God owns a complete set of books that record every transaction of a person's life, waiting to be recalled on judgment day. It may be that each of us has a recording angel who in this life is transcribing everything we do. In connection with this thought, it is well to consider Ecclesiastes 12:14: "For God will bring every work into judgment, including every secret thing, whether it is good or whether it is evil." In this final hour the books of man's works (his deeds) will be opened.

DEGREES OF PUNISHMENT

Isaiah 45:21 tells us that God is a just God, and Hebrews 2:2 advises us that "every transgression and disobedience receives a just reward." Because of the justice of God, we can be certain that He will not treat the heathen, those who have never heard the gospel of Jesus Christ, with the same judgment as the person who has listened to the message hundreds of times and rejected it. Neither will He recompense the so-called "moral citizen" (doctor, teacher, good neighbor) who has lived a comparatively decent life (though still short of the standard of God) in exactly the same way as He will Adolph Hitler, under whose regime six million of God's chosen people were slain.

Matthew 11:21-24 shows us that those with extensive opportunity to receive the truth, but who reject it, are subject to greater condemnation than those who have never heard the truth. The cities mentioned—cities in which Christ did many of his mighty works—were compared to the wicked cities of Sodom and Gomorrah, Tyre and Sidon. The residents of the cities that heard Christ will be much more severely judged because of their refusal to believe the truth. To say "it will be more tolerable for Tyre and Sidon in the day of judgment" than for Chorazin, where Christ taught and performed many miracles, establishes the fact that those who have heard the gospel and rejected it will fall into greater judgment than the homosexual sinners in Sodom.

It is imperative that every unbeliever recognize the truth that the Lord Jesus Christ will hold him accountable in proportion to the degree of opportunity he has had. The gospel of Jesus Christ is preached in almost every city and is available by radio, television, or printed page to almost everyone in the Western world. The recording angel knows and records all the times that the gospel has been heard by an individual.

To be sure, no part of hell will be a desirable place, for it is all a place of torment, but the suffering of the heathen who have never heard the gospel will not be the same as that of people who have rejected God's "so great salvation."

THE BOOKS OF LIFE

Now it is time to examine the two most important books that await every person's encounter with God. Although they are similar, they also bear significant differences.

The New Testament refers to the book of life eight different times, and although the Old Testament does not call it by that name, it does allude three times to a book in which names are written. The psalmist speaks of the righteous as having their names in "the book of the living" (Psalm 69:28), so it is a book in which righteous people have their names written.

Revelation 13:8 tells us about the other book of life—the book of life of the Lamb. "The Lamb" is without doubt the Lord Jesus Christ, for only He is the "Lamb of God who takes away the sins of the world." Because Christ came into the world to save sinners and to give them eternal life, the Lamb's book of life is the book of Jesus Christ in which are entered the names of those who have received His eternal life. (I am inclined to believe that this is a book in which only the believers who have lived since the cross have their names written.)

The above-mentioned verse indicates that during the tribulation period, people whose names are not written in the Lamb's book will worship the Antichrist. During that period all people will bear a mark. The worshipers of the Antichrist, those who have rejected the Savior, will carry the mark of the Beast—666. Those who have turned to Christ will feature a mark that is the Lamb's Father's "name written on their foreheads" (Revelation 14:1). The believers in Revelation 13:8 do not worship the Beast because their names are written in the book of the Lamb. Revelation 21:27 tells us that the only people who will enter into the Holy City are "those who are written in the Lamb's Book of Life." It is absolutely pivotal to one's eternal destiny whether or not his name is written in the Lamb's book of life!

The major difference between the two books is that the book of life seems to contain the names of *all living people*, whereas the Lamb's book of life includes only the names of those who call upon the Lamb for salvation. A second difference is that the book of life is referred to as God the Father's book in Exodus 32:33; it records all those whom God the Creator has made. It is, then, the book of the living, much like the county records book. On the other hand, the Lamb's book of life is referred to as God the Son's book (Revelation 13:8). We may conclude that this book contains the names of all those who have received the new life that the Son provides. The third and most important difference between these books is that a person may have his name blotted out of the book of life, but not out of the Lamb's book of life. According to Exodus 32:33, "The Lord said to Moses, 'Whoever has sinned against Me, I will blot him out of My book.'" It is possible, therefore, to have one's name erased from the book of life because of sin.

The Lamb's book of life is different, however. Revelation 3:5 promises, "He who overcomes shall be clothed in white garments, and I will *not blot out* his name from the Book of Life...." An overcomer in this passage is a believer who is clothed in the white garments of Christ; the Creator has imputed to him divine righteousness, and his name cannot be blotted out of the Lamb's book of life.

Primarily because a person's name *can* be blotted out of the book of life, I am convinced that the book of life and the Lamb's book of life are not the same book. As we have seen, the Lamb's book contains the names of all those who have been born again through the shed blood of the lamb, which is the guarantee that we have eternal life. Therefore we can be sure that these are two distinctly separate books. The book of life is that book in which the names of all people ever born into the world are written. If, at the time of a person's death, he has not called upon the Lord Jesus Christ for salvation, his name is blotted out of the book of life. If he *has* accepted Christ and His forgiveness of sins, his name is indelibly recorded in the Lamb's book of life, and entrance into the Holy City is guaranteed (Revelation 21:27).

GOD'S DOUBLE-CHECK

We have spent some time discussing the book of life, but in order to grasp its full importance we need to look at Revelation 20:15: "Anyone not found written in the Book of Life was cast into the lake of fire." In a sense this is God's double-check at the great white throne judgment. As a person comes forward, he is judged by the book of the law, by the books of his works, and by the Lamb's book of life. Then, just before he receives his sentence, he is given a double-check. The recording angel will refer to the book, and anyone not found written in the book of life will be thrown into the lake of fire. The Bible repeatedly contrasts two kinds of people, using such words as "believing" and "unbelieving," "saved" and "unsaved," "condemned" and "not condemned," "righteous" and "unrighteous," "just" and "unjust." This principle of contrast is maintained in names being written or not written in the book of life. In that hour there will be no hesitation or question, for a person's name is either written or not written—it must be one way or the other.

The book of life contains the names of all living souls—as though a loving God wants all people to be saved and anticipates their salvation by writing their names into the book of life. But to keep your name there, you must have your name written in the Lamb's book of life as a result of receiving the Lamb as your Lord and Savior.

ONE LAST EVENT

One awesome event recorded in Philippians is rarely mentioned in this connection, but it should be. The apostle Paul wrote:

> Therefore God also has highly exalted Him and given Him the name which is above every name, that at the name of Jesus every knee should bow, of those in heaven, and of those on earth, and of those under the earth, and that every tongue should confess that Jesus Christ is Lord, to the glory of God the Father (Philippians 2:9-11).

After giving a wonderful description of how Christ was willing to humble Himself and become "obedient to the point of death, even the death of the cross," Paul warns that there is a day coming when "every knee shall bow and every tongue confess that Jesus Christ is Lord." All the skeptics, all the infidels, all the procrastinators, and all the rejecters of Christ will acknowledge that Jesus Christ is Lord! The believers in heaven who have already bowed their knees and will to Him voluntarily, those dead who had rejected Him, and those living on the earth at His coming—all will bow to Him and acknowledge that He is Christ the Lord.

Since all men will one day bend their knee to Jesus Christ—and it will probably be right here at the close of the Great White Throne Judgment—it makes sense that it is far better to do so now, voluntarily, rather than to reject Him in this life and wait to be forced to do so that day and then be "cast into the lake of fire."

WHY WAS HELL CREATED?

The creation of an awesome place like the "lake of fire" must have been for an unusual purpose. That purpose is found in Matthew 25:41: "Then He will also say to those on the left hand, 'Depart from Me, you cursed, into the everlasting fire prepared for the devil and his angels.'" This statement made by Jesus Christ, relating to judgment day, points out that hell was created for the judgment of the devil and his angels. The apostle Peter sheds more light on this subject in 2 Peter 2:4: "If God did not spare the angels who sinned, but cast them down to hell and delivered them into chains of darkness, to be reserved for judgment...." Because the angels sinned, they are being "reserved for judgment."

Just when these angels sinned with the Devil is not absolutely certain. In the book of Job we learn that the angels were present at the original creation of the earth. It suggests that the earth was the choice dwelling-place of the angels for perhaps many years, and then Lucifer—the greatest created being, perfect in all his ways in the day he was made—rebelled against God (Ezekiel 28:15; Isaiah 14:12-15). It is impressive to notice the number of heaven's angels that fell on that fateful day. Revelation 12:4 tells us, "His tail drew a third of the stars of heaven and threw them to the earth." Think of it—one-third of the angels chose to rebel against the Most High God and to follow Lucifer, the great deceiver!

From these statements of the Lord Jesus Christ and the apostle Peter, we perceive that the lake of fire was not originally intended for man at all, but was really for the eternal punishment of supernatural beings like the devil and his angels. From the book of Revelation, particularly

20:11-15, we see that unsaved people will be cast into the lake of fire in spite of the fact that it was not originally created for them. There they will confront the indescribable misery and suffering referred to already, and be numbered among the hosts of fallen supernatural beings.

WHY PEOPLE GO TO HELL

People are dispatched to hell because they are not fit to enter heaven. The Lord Jesus Christ said in John 3:3, "Most assuredly, I say to you, unless one is born again, he cannot see the kingdom of God." "Born again" means "born from above" or "born anew," indicating that natural, physical birth is not sufficient to entitle a person to see the kingdom of God. Unless a person is born again, he or she is "corrupt in all his deeds" and unprepared for the spiritual delights of heaven; he or she must spend eternity in the lake of fire. The apostle Paul clarified this in 1 Corinthians 15:50: "Flesh and blood cannot inherit the kingdom of God; nor does corruption inherit incorruption." Our corrupt mortal bodies cannot dwell in heaven without contaminating it, for heaven is a perfect place.

A Christian has full assurance that he is going to heaven, not because he is naturally fit for heaven, but because he has been made fit by the new birth through Christ. This is not true for the ungodly person, who is "dead" toward God even though he lives physically. Consequently he can respond only to the resurrection of the dead, which leads to the second death.

THE SAVIOR IS WAITING

If Jesus Christ had not come into this world to die for our sins, we would all be sent to hell. None of us is good enough for heaven. But because He loves us, Jesus paid the penalty and accepted total punishment for all our offenses against Him, thereby making heaven available to us. It is not that

202 ◆ *The Great White Throne*

our sins are somehow minimized or overlooked; they are simply forgiven and forgotten. Those who are foolish enough to pass up this free ticket to heaven are reserving for themselves a spot in hell.

In the archives of the Supreme Court of the United States is the record of a very strange incident that took place during the term of President Andrew Jackson. A man named George Wilson was sentenced to die by hanging for a crime he had committed. Somehow the story came before the President, who granted Wilson a pardon. To everyone's amazement, Wilson tore the pardon to shreds and threw it on the floor of his prison cell. The ensuing legal argument concerned the validity of a pardon that was refused, and the question arose as to whether or not Wilson should be freed or hanged. After great deliberation, the U.S. Supreme Court ruled as follows: "A pardon is a writing, the value of which is dependent upon the acceptance by the individual for whom it is intended." It was therefore decreed by the court that George Wilson be hanged until dead—not because a pardon was not offered, but because it was not accepted.

This is a perfect picture of the sinner who hears the gospel of Jesus Christ and knows that God has written a pardon for him, yet rejects Him and thus forfeits his right to the pardon. If you are without the Savior today, it is because you choose to be. Your choice to reject Jesus Christ automatically invalidates your pardon and sentences you to the lake of fire.

Actually, you and I, during this life, are confronted with a choice. We can admit we are sinners in need of a Savior and invite Jesus Christ into our lives as Lord and Savior—or we can reject Him. In either case we will live in eternity by that choice. Those who have chosen to put their faith in Christ will "rule and reign with Him" during the thousand-year kingdom and then go on into the eternal ages with Him forever. Those who reject Him will be "cast into the lake of fire" (Revelation 20;15).

The apostle Paul has a timely warning: "Behold, now is the accepted time; behold, now is the day of salvation" (2 Corinthians 6:2).

THE LAKE OF FIRE

Those who do not have their name written in the Lamb's book of life (which guarantees that their name remains in the "book of life") will, according to Revelation 20:15, be "cast into the lake of fire," the final dwelling-place of the unbelieving dead. It is the "hell" which the Bible calls "the second death." Sinners die once, are kept in torment until the end of the thousand years, and are then resurrected to the great white throne judgment, where the Christ they refused to accept as Savior determines the degree or intensity of their eternal punishment. He then banishes them to "the lake of fire"—for eternity.

It's not a pretty sight—and not necessary, either! For the Bible says, "Believe on the Lord Jesus Christ, and you *will* be saved" (Acts 16:30).

One of the clearest offers of salvation in all the Bible came from our Lord Jesus Christ Himself:

> Most assuredly, I say to you, he who hears My word and believes in Him who sent Me has everlasting life, and shall not come into judgment, but has passed from death into life (John 5:24).

Make that right choice today!

NOTE TO BIBLE TEACHERS

This book lends itself nicely to small group Bible classes for Sunday school, or in homes. Beautiful transparencies of the charts in this book* can be ordered for a reasonable fee from:

> Visualize-It Productions
> 4263 Alta Mira Drive
> La Mesa CA 92041
> (619) 670-1894 or 660-6172

---

* As indicated in the text, a few of the charts are derived from sources other than Visualize-It Productions. These charts are not available as transparencies.

ABOUT THE AUTHOR

Tim LaHaye is an author, educator, minister, and nationally recognized speaker on family life and prophecy. His books, including *How to Study the Bible for Yourself*, have sold eight million copies and have been translated into 23 languages. He and his wife, Beverly, live and work in Washington, D.C., where he produces his daily program, "Capital Report," for radio and television.

How to Study the Bible for Yourself
by Tim LaHaye

This excellent book already has over 470,000 copies in print. It provides fascinating study helps and charts that will make personal Bible study more interesting and exciting. A three-year program is outlined for a good working knowledge of the Bible. Using this book can produce maturity in your Christian life in a relatively short period of time.

These unique techniques work for people in groups of 15 to 100 as well as on a one-on-one basis.

Other Good
Harvest House Reading

THE DAILY BIBLE
New International Version
Compiled by *F. LaGard Smith*

Unlike any other Bible you have ever read, *The Daily Bible* allows you to read the Scriptures chronologically as a powerful, uninterrupted account of God's interaction with human history.

You will see events from Creation through Revelation unfold before you like an epic novel, conveniently organized into 365 sections for daily reading. Gain a better overall perspective of Scripture by reading the Bible in the order the events occurred from the widely acclaimed New International Version.

THE SPIRIT-CONTROLLED WOMAN
by *Beverly LaHaye*

This bestselling book gives the Christian woman practical help in understanding herself and the weaknesses she encounters in her private life and in her relationships with others. Told from a woman's point of view, this book covers every stage of a woman's life.

HOW TO DEVELOP YOUR CHILD'S TEMPERAMENT
by *Beverly LaHaye*

Clearly presents ideas and concepts on how you can more successfully develop and train your child as you gain insight into his or her temperament.

Additional Books By This Author
and His Wife, Beverly LaHaye

Marriage and Family Studies

> *The Act of Marriage*
> *The Battle for the Family*
> *Spirit-Controlled Family Living*
> *How to Be Happy Though Married*
> *Sex Education Is for the Family*

Temperament Studies

Your Temperament: Discover Its Potential
Transformed Temperaments
Understanding the Male Temperament
How to Develop Your Child's Temperament
The Spirit-Controlled Woman

Victory Over Personal Problems

How to Win Over Depression
Anger Is a Choice
How to Manage Pressure
Ten Steps to Victory Over Depression
The Unhappy Gays
The Restless Woman
If a Minister Falls, Can He Be Restored?

Personal Enrichment Studies

How to Study the Bible for Yourself
Finding the Will of God
I Am a Woman By God's Design
Who But a Woman?

Prophecy and Future Things

The Beginning of the End
Revelation, Illustrated and Made Plain

Christian Social Concerns

The Battle for the Mind
The Battle for the Family
The Hidden Censors
The Race for the 21st Century
The Faith of our Founding Fathers
The Unhappy Gays

Cassette Albums Available

Spirit-Controlled Temperament (12 messages)
How to Win Over Depression (6 messages)
You and Your Family (6 messages)
The Beginning of the End (6 messages)

Family Life Cassette of the Month Club

Each month cassette messages by 38 recognized authorities on personal and family relationships give you their best experience, knowledge, and research to enhance your life. Each cassette contains a one hour message—excellent teaching material for busy people who want to learn on the run.

For information on video rentals or purchase, write or call:

Family Life Seminars
370 L'Enfant Promenade, SW
Suite 801
Washington, DC 20024
202-488-0700